TEDDY BEAR COMPANION™

The Centennial Edition—Volume III

by
Dee Hockenberry

photos by
Tom Hockenberry

PRIMEDIA

ABOUT THE AUTHOR

Dee Hockenberry has been researching and writing about teddy bears for over 20 years. This is her fourteenth book.

She is presently on the staff of two teddy bear publications. As Special Consultant for *Teddy Bear and Friends*, Dee has been instrumental in planning the magazine's celebration of the Teddy Bear Centennial.

Dee was the stamp consultant and the owner of "Frank" the Ideal bear that was chosen to be on the U.S. postage stamp in 1998. Her husband, Tom, is the photographer of the detailed pictures found in all of her works. Dee and Tom are the parents of two grown children. When not at home in Lancaster County, Pennsylvania, they can be found at teddy bear scenes all over the globe in pursuit of their shared business.

AUTHOR'S NOTE: My sincere thanks to Rick, Mindy, Maureen, Joan, Marianne, and all the staff at *Teddy Bear and Friends* for their faith, friendship, and a truly wonderful relationship.

CONTENTS

About the Author...2
Happy Birthday, Teddy...4
An Introduction to the Bear World..5

CHAPTER I	Teddy Bears 1902-2002	13
CHAPTER II	Re-Issues, Club Bear and Limited Editions	113
CHAPTER III	Artist Bears	121
CHAPTER IV	Novelty Bears and Animals	131
CHAPTER V	Mechanical Bears and Animals	151
CHAPTER VI	Barnyard Animals	158
CHAPTER VII	Birds and Fowl	163
CHAPTER VIII	Cats	170
CHAPTER IX	Dogs	180
CHAPTER X	Dressed Bears	194
CHAPTER XI	Dressed Dolls and Animals	210
CHAPTER XII	Forest and Garden Creatures	220
CHAPTER XIII	Koalas, Pandas and Polar Bears	233
CHAPTER XIV	Puppets	238
CHAPTER XV	Water Friendly Animals	243
CHAPTER XVI	Wheeled Bears and Animals	247
CHAPTER XVII	Wild Animals	253
CHAPTER XVIII	Accessories and Display	267

Index...271

ISBN 0-9715609-0-0

THE TEDDY BEAR COMPANION
THE CENTENNIAL EDITION, VOLUME III
©2002 PRIMEDIA ENTHUSIAST PUBLICATIONS, INC.
6405 Flank Drive, Harrisburg, PA 17112
(717) 657-9555

PRIMEDIA

HAPPY BIRTHDAY TEDDY

The year 2002 is a major date in the annals of teddy bear lore. This furry creature, beloved by young and old alike, is celebrating his 100th birthday. Festivities and festivals will be taking place all over the world to mark this historic occasion.

In November 1902, President Theodore Roosevelt went hunting black bears in Mississippi. On the first day of the hunt, his guides ran down a bear, but the president wasn't in position to take the shot. The guides then captured the bear, tied it to a tree, and offered the token to the president. Of course, Mr. Roosevelt considered this an unfair advantage and refused to shoot. The incident was immortalized by Washington Post political cartoonist Clifford Berryman in a cartoon titled "Drawing The Line In Mississippi."

Patric
14-1/2 inches
Gund celebrates the 100th birthday of the teddy bear with patriotic colors.

Brooklyn, New York, shopkeepers Rose and Morris Michtom were inspired by the incident and fashioned a little bear toy. They placed it in their store window and called it "Teddy's Bear." Eventually this small beginning evolved into the Ideal Toy Company, and the Michtoms became the first American teddy bear producers.

At much the same time in Germany, Richard Steiff, nephew of Steiff Company founder Margarete, also designed and made a teddy bear. Conformation was somewhat different but, for all intent and purposes, these two families, divided by an ocean, had the same idea at the same time and brought forth a plaything destined to achieve a lasting place in the world of toys.

It wasn't long before other countries followed suit and manufactured charming and innovative teddy bears. Through the past 100 years, countless companies have made sure that every child and every adult will find a bear that touches his or her heart.

The magazines, shops, museums, publishers, and, most importantly, collectors all dedicate themselves to preserving the teddy bear, who will live long after we are gone. They join with me in wishing him a happy, happy birthday!

AN INTRODUCTION TO THE BEAR WORLD

Teddy bears have been a staple in the toy world since 1902. At first the little creature was considered a child's plaything, but even in 1906, during the first teddy bear craze, adults carried teddy bears, too. For more than 20 years, since the late 1970s, most major teddy bear purchases have been by adults for their own collections.

Possibly one of the reasons for the teddy bear's perpetual popularity is that they are made in every price range and every conceivable style and color. There is truly a teddy bear for everyone. The Beanie Baby craze is a perfect example of mass-marketed bears priced for the average person. The initial cost is very affordable, although secondary market values can sometimes be very high. (Please note: Although a sampling of Beanies can be found in this guide, the fluctuation of prices forbids an accurate evaluation. Therefore no prices are given.) The pursuit of Beanie Babies has been the biggest collecting story in recent years, but only time will tell if Beanies are lasting collectibles.

When collecting any vintage product, good condition and rarity will bring the highest prices; teddy bears and collectible stuffed animals are no exception. The prices in this book are meant to be a guide and are not to be taken as absolute, since many factors enter into values. Neither the author nor the publisher assumes or accepts any responsibility for your purchases or sales.

Steiff is celebrating the teddy bear's 100th birthday. This bear is a circa 1910 example.

Bears have been made, and are still being made, in nearly every country in the world. Fine examples can be found from Australia, Austria, China, Japan, Italy, and Switzerland. However, the three countries with the largest production remain American, England, and Germany.

AMERICAN TEDDY BEARS

In 1903, in honor of Teddy Roosevelt, Morris and Rose Michtom placed a handmade bear in the window of their Brooklyn shop. The bear was so popular that demand outstripped their ability to produce, so the Michtoms organized The Ideal Novelty and Toy Company. Ideal's teddies, made in a variety of sizes, had some hallmarks: quirky features, shoebutton eyes, an embroidered or fabric nose, and longer arms and feet. In the late teens and early 1920s, the football-shaped body came into vogue. Unfortunately one rarely finds labeled Ideals, so collectors must

AN INTRODUCTION TO THE BEAR WORLD

rely on research to determine if a bear is indeed an Ideal. The company was reorganized in 1938 and the name was shortened to The Ideal Toy Co. Dolls, including Shirley Temple, were their major product. In 1982, CBS acquired the firm and teddy production ceased.

The Aetna Toy Animal Company was another early teddy bear maker. The company, which began making bears circa 1906, stamped "Aetna" on each toy's left foot. It's wonderful to find this mark intact, but because it is apt to fade or rub off, collectors should note the characteristics of Aetna's bears and study each bear's individual features. Aetna made bears with five embroidered claws and often stuffed them with shredded cork rather than the usual excelsior or kapok.

The Bruin Manufacturing Company identified its bears by a ribbon with "BMC" in gold letters affixed to the foot pad. In the absence of the ribbon, useful identification clues include eyes set deeply and inside the head seams; small ears set wide apart; and five claws. Both Aetna and Bruin made charming and quality teddies, but their written records seem to disappear after 1907, leading one to believe that production ceased then.

During the same period, The Columbia Teddy Manufacturing Co. made bears in many styles and sizes. However, their Laughing Roosevelt Bear is the only teddy that can be positively attributed to the company. This bear was made in bright gold or cinnamon fur with glass eyes. When his stomach is pressed, his mouth opens to reveal two milk-glass teeth. The mechanism can also be triggered by turning the bear's head; it is rigged by a simple but ingenious pulley system. This bear is increasingly difficult to find and is highly coveted by collectors.

E.I. Horsman, who was better known for dolls, fashioned a bear referred to as "Hecla." They also made the well-known "Billiken" that had a composition head and a mohair body. A label on the chest or foot attests to the maker, but Billiken is so distinctive that the label is hardly necessary. This was the pre-1910 period, remember, but even then companies strove to garner marketshare through innovation and unusual designs.

Other companies who made unique teddies included The Art Novelty Company, who used the patriotic colors of red, white, and blue, and the Fast Black Skirt Company who, among others, introduced the electric eye bear (shaking the right paw made the eyes light up in either red or white). Strauss made both a musical and a self-whistling bear. In addition to a full range of traditional teddies, the Dreamland Company made a "Sandy-Andy" and "Teddy Turnover" (it was a doll at one end and a teddy at the other).

Prior to World War I, American bears were made in astonishing numbers and by untold companies, and yet they are harder to find than their German counterparts. Prices are rising, but have not reached the level of Steiffs. A wise collector would concentrate on amassing a "hug" of these early bears in the best possible condition.

Post-1930 American bears are more easily located. Gund began making

AN INTRODUCTION TO THE BEAR WORLD

bears in the 1920s and continues to do so today; Winnie the Pooh is probably their biggest seller. Bears by Character and Knickerbocker are often found with tags still attached. Mohair was used, but a cotton plush is found as well, and noses tend to be metal or plastic. In 1937 the Commonwealth Organization invented a "feed me" bear, which could be fed graham crackers (crackers could be removed via the bear's zippered back).

On occasion, a collector will find a teddy with its label attached, but diligent research turns up no further information about the company or design. This phenomena piques the interest of serious collectors and inspires us to both pursue additional information and to share it with fellow arctophiles.

American Companies
Aetna: circa 1906
Applause: 1981 - present
Baker and Bigler: 1907
Bruin Manufacturing Co.: circa 1906
California Stuffed Toys: 1850-1989
Character: 1932-1983
Columbia Manufacturing Co.: circa 1907
Commonwealth: circa 1934-1937
Dakin: 1955-present
Eden Toys: 1970-present
Gund: 1898-present
Horsman, E.I. and Hecla: circa 1907
Ideal Toy Corporation: 1902-1982
Knickerbocker: 1850-present
North American Bears: 1978-present
Russ Berrie: 1963-present
Strauss: circa 1907

ENGLISH TEDDY BEARS

We can trace the history of English teddy bears to before 1910. In the beginning, many manufacturers emulated products made by Steiff, but eventually British animals and bears evolved into a unique style of their own.

In 1915 Harwin & Co. Ltd. stated that their products were as close to Steiff as possible, and examination of their catalogs confirms the assertion. Harwin's felt dolls resemble Steiff's products as well, except that the feet appear to be shorter. Confusion can arise between the two companies, especially if a collector is not aware of the similarities. In addition to dolls and bears, the Harwin line included cats, dogs, horses, and many other members of the animal kingdom. By 1920, with the war at an end and many other firms picking up produc-

AN INTRODUCTION TO THE BEAR WORLD

tion, Harwin evidently found competition too keen and went out of business.

Chad Valley began operating in 1823, but did not start making teddy bears until 1920. They also marked their bears with ear buttons, which were made of metal and inscribed, "Chad Valley British made." Other identification reads, "Chad-Valley-Aerolite-trademark." Somewhat later the company sewed fabric tags to their bears' feet. By 1938 the tag included a Royal Coat of Arms and a proclamation that Chad Valley was toy-makers to Her Majesty The Queen. The firm also made dolls with pressed-felt faces, Golliwoggs, and many animals. Large embroidered noses are characteristic of this firm's teddy bears.

Chiltern was founded in 1920. The company labeled their teddies with cloth tags sewn into the side seams. Chad Valley assumed control of Chiltern in the 1960s, so, for a span of time, the label read "Chiltern/Chad Valley."

The Farnell Company opened its doors in 1897 and began making teddies soon after Steiff in Germany and Ideal in the United States. Farnell's bears are wonderful. Though the earliest examples were not permanently marked, we assume that the "chapel window" or "webbed" claw design (five claws joined by a thread on the paw) originated with Farnell. The threads that connect the claws can best be understood by studying photographs of them.

Farnell's first trademark was a white ribbon imprinted with the words, "Farnell's/Alpha Toys/Made in England." Later they used a red, white, and blue label marked, "Farnell/Alpha/Hygienic Soft Toys." During Farnell's last four years of business, ending in 1968, the company used a square label with the legend, "This is a Farnell Quality Soft Toy Made in Hastings, England." Farnell's greatest claim to fame came as a result of Mrs. A.A. Milne's purchase, in 1920, of a Farnell bear for her son, Christopher Robin, the illustrious "Winnie-the-Pooh." In the 1990s, the Merrythought Company purchased the rights to use the Farnell name on some of their products.

Merrythought Ltd. began in 1930 and still makes quality soft toys in their Ironbridge establishment. They, too, used "chapel window" claws, though with one less claw than is found on Farnell bears. Their trademark is a wishbone and the words, "Reg'd Trademark Hygienic Merrythought Toys-made in England." Among Merrythought's most beloved products are the Cheeky and Punkinhead bears and the dog Bonzo, a cartoon character created by illustrator G.E. Studdy.

Dean's Rag Book Company was begun in London in 1903, but by 1980 had moved to Wales. The company's first product was a "rag," or cloth, book that became a nursery favorite because it was practically indestructible. The company's logo still shows two dogs trying to rip a book asunder. Dean's branched out to make "rag sheets"—fabric printed with dolls and animals that were designed to be cut, sewn, and stuffed by homemakers. From there it was a natural progression to begin making stuffed animals. One of Dean's most famous characters was Dismal Desmond, a spotted dog with a mournful countenance. In 1929, the company was granted the rights by Walt Disney to manufacture Mickey Mouse.

AN INTRODUCTION TO THE BEAR WORLD

Dean's version sports a wide-mouthed, toothy smile.

British bears can sometimes be identified by their paw pads, which were often made of rexine, a form of painted canvas; this idiosyncrasy appears to be unique to British manufacturers. Paw pads were also made of velvet. The bears were frequently stuffed with kapok in the body and excelsior in the head.

English Companies
Alresford Crafts Ltd.: 1970-1992
Canterbury: 1980-present
Chad Valley: 1820-present
Chiltern: 1924-1967
Dean's: 1903-present
Farnell: 1840-1968 (Merrythought now has the rights)
Harwin and Co.: 1914-1930
Jungle Toys: 1914-1950
Little Folk: 1976-present
Merrythought: 1919-present
Nisbet: 1953-1989
Peacock: 1953-1939
Pedigree: 1860-1988
Terry, W.J.: 1980-1924
Twyford (Action Toys) 1964-1975

GERMAN TEDDY BEARS
STEIFF

In the mid-1800s, a gentlewoman, confined to a wheelchair but possessing an active imagination and nimble fingers, made a felt pincushion in the form of an elephant. It was intended as a gift, but so impressed those who saw it that she was asked to make others. As history has revealed, this was the beginning of the Margarete Steiff Company. Margarete never married, but her nephews were active in the firm, and their progeny operate Steiff today in the town of Giengen.

One of those nephews, Richard Steiff, is credited with inventing the teddy bear in 1902. Richard saw a need for an animal toy that was jointed, like dolls. Observing animals at the circus and zoo, he thought bears and monkeys would be good candidates for jointing because they can each walk upright like humans. The prototype bear would have failed—it was thought to be too hard and heavy for children—but for an order of 3,000 pieces from a buyer in New York.

Over the years, Steiff's "barle" design evolved many times (see the illustrations). The company's methods of identifying their products evolved, too; the various markings can be important tools in dating Steiff's toys. Collectors must remember, too, that buttons have been placed in non-Steiff products. The only way to be confident about the authenticity of a Steiff is to arm oneself with as much information as possible.

BUTTONS
1902-1905: Silver-colored Elephant button; inserted by prongs
1904-1905: Silver-colored blank buttons; inserted by prongs
1905-1950: Silver-colored buttons with "Steiff" printed in raised letters with the final F trailing back; inserted by prongs
1948-1950: Bluish blank button; inserted by prongs
1949-1950: Silver-colored button with Steiff printed in block letters; inserted by prongs
1950-1968: Silver-colored button with Steiff in raised script; inserted by prongs
1968-1977: Silver-colored button with Steiff incised in script letters; inserted by a rivet
1977-present: Brass button inserted by a rivet
Note: Silver refers to the color, not the metal.

STOCK TAGS BEHIND BUTTON
1908-1925: White
1925-1934: Orange/red
1934-present: Yellow
1980-present: White used on limited replicas; otherwise yellow

CHEST TAGS
1926-1928: White with a metal rim
1928-1950: Round with a square-headed bear head at bottom; writing in brown letters
1950-1972: Round with a more rounded-headed bear at bottom; writing in blue letters
1972-present: Round tag split in half with yellow at the top and red at the bottom. The tags either have the names of the particular animal or "Original Steiff."

OTHER GERMAN COMPANIES

The Bing Works was one of many firms located in Nürnberg prior to World War II. In the first two decades of the 20th century, Bing's teddy bears resembled those made by Steiff except that their faces were a trifle flatter. Bing used a button, but it was affixed to the bear's side or arm and bore the initials "GBN" (Gebruder Bing Nürnberg). At that time Bing's animals other than teddies wore collars from which hung metal tags. The company was known for amazing mechanicals, including a line of Trip Trap bears which walked via tiny wheels in the feet. In 1920, Bing changed the emblem on the button to "BW," for Bing Works. The Bing Company ceased operations at the beginning of World War II, but in recent years has been reorganized.

Schuco, another Nürnberg firm, was founded in 1912 by partners Heinrich Muller and Heinrich Schreyer. Schreyer left the company after World War I, and a new partner, Adolf Kahn, joined the business. War again interrupted production and associations, but in 1947 Kahn's son Eric formed a new company, which operated until bankruptcy forced its closing in 1970.

Schuco produced wonderful, innovative toys. Most familiar is the yes/no line of bears and other animals. A lever in the tail allows owners to nod the head of each toy "yes" or "no." Schuco also made wheeled animals with this mechanism; examples from the 1920s usually have "Schuco" on the metal wheels. Other yes/no toys from this decade have a folded paper tag attached to the chest. Because the tag was easily torn off, it is rare to find one intact. Schuco used a special tag during America's occupation of Germany following World War II. From 1947 to 1953, a plastic tag with "Tricky" embossed on the front and "US Zone" on the reverse was attached to each toy's chest with a red ribbon. The bears from this period have wonderful faces, downward-turned paws, and cardboard-lined feet to facilitate standing. Some also contained music boxes wound from either the front or back. Toys that were five inches or smaller had Schuco's patented metal interior.

The Hermann Company has made quality soft toys since 1907, and continues to do so today. Sons of the companies' original founders have had businesses in the Sonneberg area of Germany at different periods. At the present time, Gebruder Hermann KG is in Hirschaid, where Bernard relocated, and is run by family members. Gebruder Hermann bears can be recognized from their inset snouts and paper labels (if intact). Max Hermann's company, known as Hermann Pluschtiere, operates from Coburg-Cortendorf. A marriage between the families of Hermann and Leven, another manufacturer, has now resulted in a new line of Leven Reproductions.

Other companies in Germany included Eduard Crämer, who went out of business during World War II. However this fine company has been re-established by descendants. Kersa, which operated in the 1940s and '50s, was most noted for cats and rabbits but fashioned teddies as well. Kersa identified its products with a metal tag affixed to a cardboard sole. Marks left by this symbol can be found if it has been removed. Althans began business in the 1920s and is still operating. Post-war companies include Clemens and Grisly, and the Austrian firm of Berg.

German Companies
Althans: 1920-present
Anker: 1953-1977
Berg: 1946-present

AN INTRODUCTION TO THE BEAR WORLD

Bing: 1860-1932 (recently resurrected)
Clemens: 1947-present
Crämer: 1885-mid 1950s (recently resurrected)
Diem: 1896-mid 1950s
Gebr. Hermann: 1948-present (family business established in 1913)
Hermann Spielwaren: 1979-present (family business established in 1913)
Fechter: 1946-1978
Jopi: 1910-late 1950s
Kersa: 1925-present
Petz: 1948-1974
Schuco: 1912-1976
Steiff: 1877-present
Süssenguth: circa 1920

INTERNATIONAL TEDDIES

Of course bears have been produced by many firms all over the world. Some of the bruins you may encounter are listed below.

AUSTRALIA
Berlex: 1950s-1970
Emil Pity Ltd.: 1930s-1970s
Joy Toys: 1920-1971
Lindee: 1944-1976
Verna: 1941-1980s

CHINA
Shanghai Doll Factory: 1970-present

FRANCE
Aux Nations: 1964-present
Fadap: 1925-1978
M. Pintel Fils: 1913-1976
Thiennot: 1919-1993

ITALY
Trudy: 1949-present

SWITZERLAND
MCZ (Mutzli-Felpa): 1950-1990

The bears and animals in this book are, as much as possible, in chronological order and not necessarily by manufacturer or country of origin.

TEDDY BEARS 1902 - 2002 • CHAPTER I

The conformation, choice of materials for all components, and the methods for identification changed gradually over the years of the teddy bear's existence. Variations can best be seen by studying the photographs and descriptions for each bruin. Every country had (and has) its own choice of design, as well, and with enough handling of teddies, one can become proficient in telling the difference.

STEIFF ROD BEAR

15 inches

All jointed by metal rods; mohair felt pads; shoe button eyes; firmly stuffed; sealing wax nose; circa 1902/1903/1904.

This style of bear, modified somewhat in this 1904 example, was first designed in 1902 and introduced in 1903. Jointing was by strings in the first products.

Marks: Elephant button

Price: $30,000

Photo courtesy of Dottie Ayers

STEIFF TEDDY BEAR
29 inches
Cinnamon mohair; shoe button eyes; felt pads; excelsior stuffed; center head seam; all jointed; mint; circa 1906.

Marks: FF button

Price: $25,000 up

Photo courtesy of Dottie Ayers

AMERICAN TEDDY BEAR
18 inches
Gold mohair; glass eyes; open mouth with two glass teeth that closes when head is turned or stomach is pressed; felt pads; excelsior stuffed; all jointed; Laughing Roosevelt Bear produced by the Columbia Manufacturing Co.; shown with Teddy Roosevelt watch fob; 1906.

Marks: None

Price: $2,000 - 2,500

STEIFF TEDDY BEAR
13 inches
Mohair; shoe button eyes; felt pads; excelsior stuffed; all jointed; near mint; circa 1907.

Marks: Blank button

Price: $4,500

CHAPTER I

STEIFF TEDDY BEAR

16 inches

Mohair; shoe button eyes; felt pads; excelsior stuffed; all jointed; center seam on head; mint; circa 1907.

Marks: None

Price: $12,000 - $15,000

IDEAL TEDDY BEAR *FRANK*

10 inches

Gold mohair; shoe button eyes; felt pads (replaced on feet;) excelsior stuffed; all jointed; excellent condition; circa 1906.

Marks: None

Price: Because of the provenance of his being used for a U.S. Postage Stamp (issued in 1998), an accurate evaluation us difficult to determine.

AMERICAN TEDDY BEAR

15 inches

Gold mohair; glass eyes; felt pads; cork stuffed; all jointed; made by the Aetna Co.; good condition; circa 1907.

Marks: None

Price: $900 up

AMERICAN AETNA TEDDY BEAR

20 inches

Gold mohair; glass eyes; floss nose, mouth and claws; cork stuffed; felt pads; (feet lined with stiff cardboard); all jointed; circa 1907.

Marks: None

Price: $2,000 - $2,500

CHAPTER I

AMERICAN BRUIN TEDDY BEAR

13 inches

Apricot mohair; glass eyes; felt pads; excelsior stuffed; all jointed; near mint; circa 1907.

Marks: Label on right foot

Price: Sold at Christie's, London, in 1996 for approximately $6,600.

Photo courtesy of Christie's

AMERICAN TEDDY BEAR

20 inches

Very worn mohair; shoe button eyes; felt pads; excelsior stuffed; all jointed; original rough rider costume; shoes added; circa 1907.

Price: Worn condition precludes exact pricing (what the market will bear - more for charm and historical significance).

Photo courtesy of Dottie Ayers

AMERICAN TEDDY BEAR

12 inches

Gold mohair; glass eyes; felt pads; excelsior stuffed; twill fabric nose; mint; circa 1907.

Marks: None

Price: $1,000 - $1,200

LAUGHING ROOSEVELT TEDDY BEAR
14 inches
Rust mohair; glass eyes; felt pads; open wooden mouth and two milk glass teeth; pull string under chin to open and close mouth; all jointed; excelsior stuffed; excellent condition; Columbia Mfg. Co.; circa 1907.

Marks: None
Price: $2,400

LAUGHING ROOSEVELT TEDDY BEAR
16 inches
Mohair; glass eyes; felt pads; excelsior stuffed; wooden mouth with two milk teeth; mouth opens and closes by turning head or pressing tummy; near mint mohair; wear to pads; made by Columbia Mfg. Co.; circa 1907.

Marks: None
Price: $2,500

AMERICAN HECLA TEDDY BEAR
20 inches
White mohair; shoe button eyes; felt pads; excelsior stuffed; all jointed; near mint; circa 1907.

Marks: None
Price: $2,500

CHAPTER I

IDEAL TEDDY BEAR
12 inches
Mohair; shoe button eyes; cloth nose; felt pads; excelsior stuffed; all jointed; mint; circa 1907.

Marks: None

Price: $1,500

AMERICAN IDEAL TEDDY BEAR
13 inches
Tan mohair; shoe button eyes; felt pads; excelsior stuffed; mint; circa 1907.

Marks: None

Price: $1,500

AMERICAN IDEAL TEDDY BEAR
16 inches
Tan mohair; shoe button eyes; felt pads; excelsior stuffed; all jointed; excellent condition; circa 1907.

Marks: None

Price: $1,200

TEDDY BEARS 1902-2000

STEIFF TEDDY BEAR

25 inches

Silver mohair; shoe button eyes; felt pads; excelsior stuffed; all jointed; center head seam; provenance of having belonged to Elizabeth Brown of Coventry, England; mint; circa 1908.

Marks: FF button

Price: $24,500 with photo

Photo of Elizabeth Brown with her center seam Steiff teddy.

CHAPTER I

STEIFF TEDDY BEAR
15 inches
Gold mohair; shoe button eyes; felt pads; growler; all jointed; slight wear; circa 1908.

Marks: None

Price: Approximately $7,200 at Christie's, London, auction in 1999.

Photo courtesy of Christie's

STEIFF TEDDY BEAR
20 inches
Cinnamon mohair; shoe button eyes; felt pads; excelsior stuffed; all jointed; some wear to pads; circa 1908.

Marks; None

Price: $10,000

BING TEDDY BEAR
13 inches
Mohair; shoe button eyes; felt pads; excelsior stuffed; all jointed; near mint; circa 1908.

Marks: G B N (Gebrüder Bing Nürnberg) button

Price: $2,500

GERMAN BING TEDDY BEAR
20 inches
Gold mohair; shoe button eyes; felt pads; excelsior stuffed; all jointed; mint; circa 1908.

Marks: None

Price: $3,500 up

AMERICAN TEDDY BEAR WITH PROVENANCE
30 inches
Tan mohair; replaced eyes; leather pads (original); excelsior stuffed; all jointed; near mint; signed on foot "Sylvia Clegg, Calumet, Michigan 1903;" this has been authenticated by an expert as original, possibly her birth date; bear circa 1908.

Marks: As stated

Price: $4,500 up

AMERICAN TEDDY BEAR
14 inches
Gold mohair; shoe button eyes; felt pads; excelsior stuffed; all jointed; shows some wear; possibly Ideal; circa 1908.

Marks: None

Price: $595

CHAPTER I

AMERICAN BRUIN TEDDY BEAR
17 inches
Off-white mohair; glass eyes; felt pads; excelsior and cotton stuffed; all jointed; good condition; circa 1908.

Marks: None

Price: $1,800 up

IDEAL AMERICAN TEDDY BEAR
12 inches
Cinnamon mohair; shoe button eyes; felt pads; excelsior stuffed; all jointed; shows some wear; circa 1909.

Marks: None

Price: $400-$500

AMERICAN TEDDY BEAR
15 inches
Gold mohair; replaced pads; glass eyes; fabric nose; excellent condition; possibly Ideal; circa 1909.

Marks: None

Price: $900

TEDDY BEARS 1902-2000

AMERICAN TEDDY BEAR

24 inches

Mohair; shoe button eyes; felt pads; excelsior stuffed; all jointed; near mint; circa 1910.

Marks: None

Price: $2,700

STEIFF TEDDY BEAR

10 inches

Cinnamon mohair; shoe button eyes; felt pads; excelsior stuffed; all jointed; mint; circa 1910.

Marks: FF button

Price: Approximately $6,500 at Christie's, London, auction in 1999.

STEIFF ROLY POLY BEAR

7 inches

Blond mohair; shoe button eyes; excelsior stuffed; jointed head and arms; weighted base with rattle; shows some wear; circa 1909.

Marks: FF button

Price: Approximately $14,250 at Christie's, London, auction in 1999.

Photo courtesy of Christie's

CHAPTER I

STEIFF TEDDY BEARS
12 inches
Cinnamon mohair; shoe button eyes; felt pads; excelsior stuffed; all jointed; squeakers; mint; circa 1910.

Marks: FF button

Price: Approximately $14,250 at Christie's, London, auction in 1999.

Photo courtesy of Christie's

TEDDY BEARS 1902-2000

STEIFF TEDDY BEAR
13 inches
Off-white mohair; shoe button eyes; felt pads; excelsior stuffed; all jointed; good condition; circa 1910.

Marks: None

Price: $1,850

STEIFF MUZZLE TEDDY BEAR
16 inches
Tan mohair; shoe button eyes; excelsior stuffed; all jointed; near mint; circa 1910.

Price: $10,000 up

STEIFF TEDDY BEAR
20 inches
White mohair; shoe button eyes; felt pads; excelsior stuffed; all jointed; mint; circa 1910.

Marks: FF button

Price: $16,000

BING TEDDY BEAR
12 inches
Pale copper mohair; shoe button eyes; felt pads; excelsior stuffed; all jointed; excellent condition; circa 1910.

Marks: None

Price: $1,425

GERMAN TEDDY BEAR
24 inches
Light cinnamon mohair; shoe button eyes; replaced felt pads; excelsior stuffed; all jointed; some mohair wear; appears to be made by Bing; circa 1910.

Marks: None

Price: $1,950-$2,200

AMERICAN TEDDY BEAR
10 inches
Pale cinnamon mohair; shoe button eyes; felt pads; excelsior stuffed; all jointed; circa 1910.

Marks: None

Price: $450

TEDDY BEARS 1902-2000

AMERICAN TEDDY BEAR

12 inches

Gold mohair; shoe button eyes; felt pads; unusual because it is the first early American bear seen with a tail that moves back and forth; near mint; circa 1910.

Marks: None

Price: $750

AMERICAN TEDDY BEAR

13 inches

Gold bristly mohair; glass eyes; felt pads; excelsior stuffed; all jointed; large ears; excellent condition; clothes not original; circa 1910.

Marks: None

Price: $950-$1,000

AMERICAN TEDDY BEAR

13 inches

Gold mohair; shoe button eyes; felt pads; excelsior stuffed; all jointed; excellent condition; circa 1910.

Marks: None

Price: $850-$900

CHAPTER I

GERMAN TEDDY BEAR

22 inches

Mohair; felt pads; shoe button eyes; excelsior stuffed; all jointed; possible Bing; near mint; circa 1910.

Marks: None

Price: $2,600

AMERICAN TWINS

14 inches

Tan mohair; shoe button eyes; felt pads; all jointed; excellent condition; shown with book that featured their portrait on the cover; circa 1910.

Marks: None

Price: $2,800 pair

AMERICAN TEDDY BEAR
18 inches
Tan mohair; glass eyes; felt pads; excelsior stuffed; all jointed; football body; possibly Ideal; near mint; circa 1910.

Marks: None

Price: $900

AMERICAN TEDDY BEAR
14 inches
Cinnamon gold mohair; felt pads; shoe button eyes; excelsior and soft stuffed; all jointed; some mohair loss; circa 1910.

Marks: None

Price: $895

AMERICAN TEDDY BEAR
14 inches
Tan mohair; shoe button eyes; felt pads; excelsior stuffed; all jointed; circa 1910.

Marks: None

Price: $850

CHAPTER I

AMERICAN TEDDY BEAR
14 inches
Mohair; shoe button eyes; felt pads; excelsior stuffed; all jointed; mint; circa 1910.

Marks: None

Price: $1,300

AMERICAN TEDDY BEAR
15 inches
Gold mohair; shoe button eyes; felt pads; excelsior stuffed; all jointed; near mint; circa 1910.

Marks: None

Price: $895

AMERICAN TEDDY BEAR
15 inches
White mohair; shoe button eyes; felt pads; excelsior stuffed; all jointed; near mint; circa 1910.

Marks: None

Price: $600

AMERICAN TEDDY BEAR

18 inches

Tan mohair; felt pads; shoe button eyes; excelsior stuffed; all jointed; near mint; circa 1910.

Marks: None

Price: $1,500

AMERICAN TEDDY BEAR

15-1/2 inches

Gold mohair; shoe button eyes; felt pads; excelsior stuffed; all jointed; circa 1910.

Marks: None

Price: $500-$550

Gail Norris Collection

CHAPTER I

STEIFF BLACK TEDDY BEAR
20 inches
Black curly mohair; shoe button eyes backed by red felt; felt pads; excelsior stuffed; all jointed; mint; circa 1912.
Price: $40,000

Rod bear in photo is described elsewhere.

Photo courtesy of Dottie Ayers

TEDDY BEARS 1902-2000

GERMAN TEDDY BEAR
11 inches
Cinnamon mohair; shoe button eyes; felt pads; excelsior stuffed; all jointed; near mint; circa 1912.

Marks: None

Price: $1,050

AMERICAN TEDDY BEAR
16 inches
Cinnamon mohair; glass eyes; felt pads; excelsior stuffed; all jointed; shows wear; circa 1912.

Marks: None

Price: $400-$500

AMERICAN TEDDY BEAR
22 inches
Mohair; excelsior and soft stuffed; glass eyes; all jointed; excellent condition; circa 1912.

Marks: None

Price: $995 up

CHAPTER I

ENGLISH TEDDY BEAR
27 inches
Made by William J. Terry Co.; gold mohair; glass eyes; fabric pads; excelsior stuffed; all jointed; near mint; circa 1913.

Marks: None

Price: $3,200 up

GERMAN TEDDY BEAR
15 inches
Gold mohair; glass eyes; felt pads; excelsior stuffed; all jointed; circa 1915.

Marks: None

Price: $995

BING TEDDY BEAR
16 inches
Mohair; shoe button eyes; felt pads; excelsior stuffed; all jointed; near mint; circa 1915.

Marks: None

Price: $2,400

TEDDY BEAR
24 inches

Black mohair (faded to green in places); shoe button eyes; velvet pads; very pronounced hump; all jointed; excellent condition; maker unknown; circa 1915.

Marks: None

Price: $2,200

AMERICAN TEDDY BEAR
15 inches

Bronze mohair; felt pads; replaced glass eyes; excelsior stuffed; all jointed; excellent condition; maker unknown; circa 1915.

Marks: None

Price: $600-$750

AMERICAN TEDDY BEAR
20 inches

Tan mohair; felt pads; glass eyes; excelsior stuffed; all jointed; football shaped body; possibly Ideal; excellent condition; circa 1915.

Marks: None

Price: $400-450

CHAPTER I

AMERICAN TEDDY BEAR

23 inches

Tan mohair; shoe button eyes; replaced felt pads; excelsior stuffed; all jointed; considered a stick bear because of straight limbs; circa 1915.

Marks: None

Price: $450-$500

AMERICAN TEDDY BEAR

25 inches

Gold mohair; glass eyes; felt pads; excelsior stuffed; football shaped body; all jointed; near mint; circa 1915.

Marks: None

Price: $850

FARNELL TEDDY BEAR
11 inches
Gold mohair; felt pads; shoe button eyes; excelsior stuffed; all jointed; excellent condition; circa 1915.

Marks: None

Price: $1,700

FARNELL TEDDY BEAR
13 inches
Mohair; shoe button eyes; excelsior and kapok stuffed; all jointed; near mint; circa 1915.

Marks: None

Price: $2,200

FARNELL TEDDY BEAR
13 inches
Gold mohair; shoe button eyes; felt pads; excelsior and kapok stuffed; circa 1915.

Marks: None

Price: $1,700

CHAPTER I

FARNELL TEDDY BEAR
14 inches

Off-white mohair; shoe button eyes; foot pads (stitched and webbed on the hands); excelsior and kapok stuffed; all jointed; circa 1915.

Marks: None

Price: $2,400

FARNELL TEDDY BEAR
16 inches

Gold mohair; shoe button eyes; felt pads; webbed paw pads; excelsior and kapok stuffed; near mint; circa 1915.

Marks: None

Price: $2,000

FARNELL TEDDY BEAR
21 inches

Blond mohair; glass eyes; felt pads (webbed on hands); excelsior and kapok stuffed; all jointed; mint; circa 1915.

Marks: None

Price: $3,500

TEDDY BEARS 1902-2000

AMERICAN TEDDY BEAR
24 inches
Gold mohair; glass eyes; felt pads; football-shaped body; near mint; circa 1918.

Marks: None

Price: $700

AMERICAN TEDDY BEAR
26 inches
Gold mohair; shoe button eyes; felt pads (bottoms replaced); excelsior stuffed; all jointed; football-shaped body with stick type limbs; good condition; circa 1918.

Marks: None

Price: $650-$750

AMERICAN TEDDY BEAR
24 inches
Tan mohair; glass eyes; felt pads; football-shaped body; all jointed; excellent conditions; circa 1918.

Marks: None

Price: $650-700

CHAPTER I

AMERICAN TEDDY BEAR
20 inches

Gold mohair; glass eyes; replaced felt pads; football-shaped body; all jointed; near mint; circa 1918.

Marks: None

Price: $650-700

GERMAN BING TEDDY BEAR
20 inches

Pale gold mohair; shoe button eyes; felt pads (bottom cardboard lined); excelsior stuffed; all jointed; near mint; circa 1919.

Marks: None

Price: $2,500

TEDDY BEARS 1902-2000

GERMAN TEDDY BEAR
17 inches
Gold mohair; shoe button eyes; the felt pads were replaced long ago with leather; excelsior stuffed; all jointed; possibly made by Bing; circa 1919.

Marks: None

Price: $1,000 up

AMERICAN TEDDY BEAR
15 inches
Short mohair; glass eyes; felt pads; excelsior stuffed; stick figure construction; all jointed; circa 1915.

Marks: None

Price: $325-$350

Gail Norris Collection

CHAPTER I

GERMAN STRUNZ TEDDY BEAR
14 inches
Gold mohair; shoe button eyes; felt pads; excelsior stuffed; all jointed; shows some wear; circa 1919.

Marks: None

Price: Sold at Christie's, London, in 1996 for approximately $1,100.

Photo courtesy of Christie's

STEIFF TEDDY BEAR
10 inches
Gold mohair; glass eyes; felt pads; excelsior stuffed; all jointed; excellent condition; 1920s.

Marks: None

Price: $1,450

STEIFF TEDDY BEAR
12 inches
Gold mohair; glass eyes; felt pads; excelsior stuffed; all jointed; excellent condition; 1920s.

Marks: Printed FF button

Price: $2,900

TEDDY BEARS 1902-2000

STEIFF TEDDY BEAR

16 inches

Gold mohair; glass eyes; felt pads; excelsior stuffed; mint; 1920s.

Marks: FF button

Price: $3,500

STEIFF TEDDY BEAR

18 inches

White mohair; glass eyes; felt pads; growler; excelsior stuffed; all jointed; mint; circa 1920.

Marks: FF button

Price: $4,000

CHAPTER I

STEIFF TEDDY BEAR
30 inches
Gold mohair; glass eyes; felt pads; excelsior stuffed; all jointed; mint; 1920s.

Marks: FF button

Price: $12,000-$13,000

GERMAN BING TEDDY BEAR
8-1/4 inches

Cinnamon brown alpaca; shoe button eyes; felt pads; excelsior stuffed; all jointed; excellent condition; circa 1920.

Marks: Button on left side

Price: $995

BING TEDDY BEAR
13 inches

Cinnamon mohair; glass eyes; replaced pads; excelsior stuffed; all jointed; near mint; circa 1920.

Marks: None

Price: $1,400-$1,500

BING TEDDY BEAR
20 inches

Gold mohair; felt pads; excelsior stuffed; all jointed; circa 1920.

Marks: None

Price: $2,200

CHAPTER I

BING TEDDY BEAR

23 inches (standing bear)

Blond mohair; glass eyes; felt pads; growler; excelsior stuffed; all jointed; near mint; circa 1920.

Marks: None

Price: Sold in 1996 at Christie's, London, for approximately $7,500.

Photo courtesy of Christie's

BING TEDDY BEAR

26 inches (sitting bear)

Brown tipped blond mohair; glass eyes; felt pads; growler; excelsior stuffed; tipping is faded; patches to pads; circa 1920.

Marks: None

Price: Sold at Christie's, London, in 1996 for approximately $6,000.

GERMAN TEDDY BEAR

28 inches

Gold mohair; felt pads; glass eyes; painted orange on back; excelsior stuffed; all jointed; near mint; appears to be made by Bing; circa 1920.

Marks: None

Price: $3,700-$4,000

TEDDY BEARS 1902-2000

BING TEDDY BEAR
24 inches
Cream and brown tipped mohair (faded); glass eyes (replaced); replaced felt pads; restitched nose and mouth; excelsior stuffed; all jointed; excellent condition; circa 1920.

Marks: Metal B.W. button (Bing Werke) on right arm

Price: $3,500-$4,000

GERMAN TEDDY BEAR
18 inches
Gold bristly mohair; shoe button eyes; replaced leather pads; excelsior stuffed; all jointed; imaginatively dressed in felt clothes not original to bear (probably belonged to a rabbit); worn condition; maker unknown; circa 1920.

Marks: None

Price: $650-$750

GERMAN TEDDY BEAR
22 inches
Dark gold mohair; shoe button eyes; felt pads; nose and mouth reworked; excelsior stuffed; all jointed; near mint; circa 1920.

Marks: None

Price: $850-$900

CHAPTER I

EDWARD CRÄMER TEDDY BEAR
14 inches
Short blonde mohair; glass eyes; felt pads; excelsior stuffed; some wear on forehead and arms; circa 1920.

Price: Sold at Christie's, London, in 1996 for approximately $3,000.

Photo courtesy of Christie's

HELVETIC TEDDY BEAR
14 inches
Long off-white mohair (traces of green can be detected); felt pads; oversize glass eyes; excelsior stuffed; all jointed; holes in pads; mohair loss on muzzle and stomach; music box activated by squeezing the back and stomach; Swiss made; circa 1920.

Marks: None

Price: $800 up

BELLOWS MUSICAL JOPI TEDDY BEAR
16 inches
Long white mohair; glass eyes; felt pads; excelsior stuffed; all jointed; squeeze type music box; excellent condition; circa 1920.

Marks: None

Price: $2,800

TEDDY BEARS 1902-2000

SCHUCO YES/NO TEDDIES
16 and 11 inches

Gold mohair; shoe button eyes; rayon pads; excelsior stuffed; excellent condition; circa 1920.

Marks: None

Price: 16 inch-$1,500, 11 inch-$1,000

SCHUCO TEDDY BEAR
9 inches

Gold mohair; rayon pads; amber glass faceted eyes (available only be special order); excelsior stuffed; all jointed; shows some mohair wear; 1920s.

Marks: None

Price: $875

CHAPTER I

EUROPEAN TEDDY BEAR
20 inches

Gold mohair; glass eyes; replaced felt pads; excelsior stuffed; all jointed; worn condition; dress added; circa 1920.

Marks: None

Price: $150-200

AMERICAN TEDDY BEAR
19 inches

Gold mohair; felt pads; glass eyes; excelsior stuffed; all jointed; excellent condition; maker unknown; circa 1920.

Marks: None

Price: $400-$450

AMERICAN TEDDY BEAR
14 inches

Apricot mohair; glass eyes; replaced fabric pads; excelsior stuffed; all jointed; shows some wear; sweater added; circa 1920.

Marks: None

Price: $275

STICK FIGURE TEDDY BEAR

16 inches

Green mohair; glass eyes; replaced felt pads; excelsior stuffed; unusually large ears; all jointed; stick-like limbs; excellent condition; circa 1920.

Marks: None

Price: $175-$225

ENGLISH FARNELL TEDDY BEAR

20 inches

Pale gold mohair; glass eyes; felt pads with typical webbed paws; softly stuffed kapok with excelsior in muzzle area; all jointed; mohair wear on sides under arms; circa 1920.

Marks: None

Price: $1,800 up

ENGLISH ALPHA FARNELL TEDDY BEAR

18 inches

Tan mohair; glass eyes; replaced felt pads; excelsior and kapok stuffed; all jointed; near mint; circa 1920.

Marks: None

Price: $1,650

ENGLISH TEDDY TOY COMPANY TEDDY BEAR

23 inches

Gold mohair; glass eyes; felt pads (cardboard lined on feet); all jointed; mint; circa 1920.

Marks: None

Price: Sold at Christie's, London, in 1999 for approximately $3,400.

Photo courtesy of Christie's

WILLIAM J. TERRY TEDDY BEAR

16 inches

Coppery mohair; large glass eyes; felt pads; paw pads embroidered with claws; foot pads cardboard lined; excelsior and kapok stuffed; all jointed; circa 1920.

Marks: None

Price: $2,000-$2,500

WILLIAM J. TERRY TEDDY BEAR

19 inches

Light gold mohair; glass eyes; linen pads (cardboard lined soles and webbed on the hands); slight wear; circa 1920.

Marks: None

Price: Sold at Christie's, London, in 1999 for approximately $3,800.

Photo courtesy of Christie's

CHAPTER I

ENGLISH CHAD VALLEY CUBBY BEAR

13 inches (sitting)
Alpaca; glass eyes; felt pads; kapok stuffed; swivel head and arms; excellent condition; circa 1920s.

Marks: Celluloid button on back

Price: $900

CHAD VALLEY CIRCA 1925 HANG TAG

TEDDY BEARS 1902-2000

BING TEDDY BEAR
10 inches

Gold mohair; glass eyes; felt pads; excelsior stuffed; all jointed; excellent condition; circa 1925.

Marks: None

Price: $1,195

SCHUCO YES/NO TEDDY BEAR
18 inches

Cream mohair tipped with purple; glass eyes; felt pads; excelsior pads; all jointed; excellent condition; circa 1925.

Marks: None

Price: Sold at Christie's, London, in 1996 for approximately $3,400.

Photo courtesy of Christie's

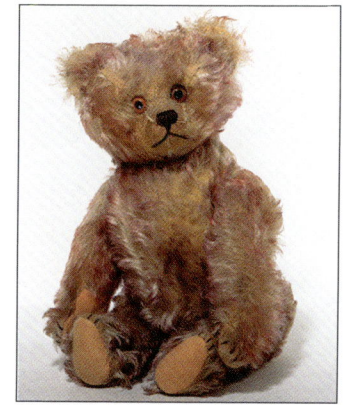

SCHUCO YES/NO TEDDY BEAR
16 inches

Bright gold mohair; felt pads; shoe button eyes; excelsior stuffed; all jointed; excellent condition; circa 1925.

Marks: None

Price: $1,500 up

CHAPTER I

SCHUCO YES/NO TEDDY BEAR
14 inches

Short gold mohair; replaced felt pads (original were rayon); excelsior stuffed; amber faceted glass eyes (these were available by special order only); all jointed; shows wear; circa 1925.

Marks: None

Price: $1,599 up

Gail Norris Collection

FARNELL TEDDY BEAR
15 inches

Off-white mohair; glass eyes; cloth pads (stitched and webbed on hands); excelsior and kapok stuffed; all jointed; circa 1925.

Marks: None

Price: $2,500

ENGLISH WILLIAM TERRY BEAR
16 inches

Mohair; felt pads; glass eyes; excelsior and kapok stuffed; all jointed; near mint; circa 1925. This bear has provenance of owner and comes with several photos and negatives.

Price: $2,000 up

ENGLISH WILLIAM J. TERRY TEDDY BEAR

17 inches

Cinnamon gold mohair; glass eyes; cloth pads (stitched and webbed on hands); excelsior and kapok stuffed; circa 1925.

Marks: None

Price: $2,900 up

SCHUCO YES/NO TEDDY BEAR

14 inches

Dark blue mohair; shoe button eyes; linen pads; excelsior stuffed; all jointed; near mint; rare; circa 1926.

Marks: Original tag on left arm

Price: Sold at Christie's, London, in 1996 for approximately $18,500.

Photo courtesy of Christie's

CHAPTER I

STEIFF *PETSY* TEDDY BEAR
12 inches

Brown-tipped cream mohair; blue glass eyes; rose embroidered nose, mouth and claws; felt pads; wired ears; excelsior stuffed; all jointed; excellent condition; 1928.

Marks: FF button; trace of orange stock tag

Price: $8,900

BELLOWS MUSICAL HELVETIC TEDDY BEAR
15 inches

Apricot mohair; oversize glass eyes; felt pads; excelsior stuffed; all jointed; squeeze type music box; mint; circa 1928.

Side view of Helvetic Bear (right) showing the pronounced upward turning nose. This is a distinct profile.

Marks: None

Price: $2,900

MORITZ PAPPE BABY-BÄRS

8 and 11 inches

Blond mohair; glass eyes with felt backs; orange felt mouths; velvet pads; excelsior stuffed; all jointed; near mint; rare; circa 1928.

Marks: None

Price: Sold at Christie's, London, in 1996 for approximately $1,900 and 4,500.

Photo courtesy of Christie's

STEIFF *PETSY* BEAR BEAR

24 inches

Reddish brown tips on cream mohair; felt pads; blue glass eyes; pinky red nose, mouth, and claws; large wired ears; seamed between ears and center of head; all jointed; 1929.

Marks: FF button; trace of orange stock tag

Price: $15,000 up

CHAPTER I

BELLOWS MUSICAL HELVETIC TEDDY BEAR

12 inches

Apricot mohair; oversized glass eyes; felt pads; excelsior stuffed; squeeze type music movement; all jointed; shows some wear; circa 1929.

Marks: None

Price: $1,600 up

Gail Norris Collection

CHAD VALLEY DUTCH TEDDY BEAR

12 inches

Wool plush; tri-colored eyes; soft stuffed; swivel head; near mint; circa 1930.

Marks: None

Price: $1,000

GERMAN TEDDY BEAR

17 inches

Gold mohair; glass eyes; felt pads; excelsior and cotton stuffed; all jointed; squeaker; near mint; appears to made by Moritz Pappe; circa 1930.

Marks: None

Price: $450-$500

TEDDY BEARS 1902-2000

KNICKERBOCKER TEDDY BEARS
18 inches

Gold and brown mohair; glass eyes; metal noses; excelsior stuffed; felt pads; all jointed; circa 1930.

Marks: None

Price: $325-$400 each

Gail Norris Collection

KNICKERBOCKER TEDDY BEAR
17 inches

Brown mohair; glass eyes; metal nose; felt pads; excelsior and cotton stuffed; all jointed; mint; 1930.

Marks: None

Price: $375

CHAPTER 1

AMERICAN TEDDY BEAR
17 inches
Gray mohair; felt pads; replaced eyes; soft stuffed; maker unknown; mint; late 1930s.

Marks: None

Price: $650

CHAD VALLEY TEDDY BEAR
25 inches
Mohair; glass eyes; replaced pads; excelsior and kapok stuffed; all jointed; near mint; circa 1930.

Marks: Label on foot; celluloid button in ear

Price: $1,300 up

CHAD VALLEY TEDDY BEAR
28 inches
Mohair; glass eyes; kapok and excelsior stuffed; patched hand pads; all jointed; excellent condition; circa 1930.

Marks: Label on foot

Price: $1,300 up

TEDDY BEARS 1902-2000

BILLY WINKY DEAN'S TEDDY BEAR
18 inches
Blond mohair; glass eyes; felt pads; all jointed; shows some wear; made by Dean's of England; circa 1930.

Marks: None

Price: Sold at Christie's, London, in 1999 for approximately $550.

DEAN'S TEDDY BEAR CUB
18 inches
Blond mohair; glass eyes; felt pads; all jointed; near mint; circa 1930.

Marks: Label on foot

Price: Sold at Christie's, London, in 1999 for approximately $1,050.

Photo courtesy of Christie's

CHAPTER I

ENGLISH CHILTERN TEDDY BEAR

15 inches

Gold mohair; clipped muzzle; glass eyes; kapok and excelsior stuffed; velvet paw pads (bottom reinforced with cardboard); all jointed; mint; circa 1930.

Marks: None

Price: $1,100-$1200

ENGLISH TEDDY BEAR

22 inches

Gold mohair; repaired felt pads; brown glass eyes; excelsior and kapok stuffed; all jointed; made by Farnell; circa 1930.

Marks: None

Price: $1,500-$1,600

ENGLISH FARNELL TEDDY BEAR

18 inches

Black mohair; excelsior and kapok stuffed; clear glass eyes painted rose on the back; pink embroidered nose, mouth, and five joined claws; all jointed; minor mohair loss; circa 1930.

Marks: None

Price: $1,300 up

ENGLISH FARNELL TEDDY BEAR

20 inches

Off-white mohair; glass eyes; linen pads; excelsior and kapok stuffed; all jointed; mended muzzle area; straining on pads; circa 1930.

Marks: None

Price: $1,300-$1,400

MERRYTHOUGHT TEDDY BEAR

19 inches

Lime green silk plush; glass eyes; felt pads (webbed on front paws); excelsior and kapok stuffed; all jointed; near mint; circa 1930.

Marks: Label on foot

Price: $1,600

CHAPTER I

MERRYTHOUGHT TEDDY BEAR

15 inches

Red silk plush; red felt pads; webbed claws on palms; glass eyes; kapok stuffed; all jointed; circa 1930.

Marks: Celluloid button; label on foot

Price: $800 up

Donna McPherson Collection

ENGLISH MERRYTHOUGHT BINGIE BEAR

14 inches (sitting)

Blond mohair; replaced felt pads; glass eyes; swivel head and arms; kapok stuffed; minor mohair loss; hard to find; circa 1930.

Marks: Tag on leg

Price: $800

TEDDY BEARS 1902-2000

ENGLISH MERRYTHOUGHT TEDDY BEAR

19 inches

Gold mohair; felt pads; glass eyes; four joined claws; kapok and excelsior stuffed; all jointed; mint condition; circa 1930.

Marks: Celluloid button in right ear; paper hang tag

Price: $1,600-$1,700

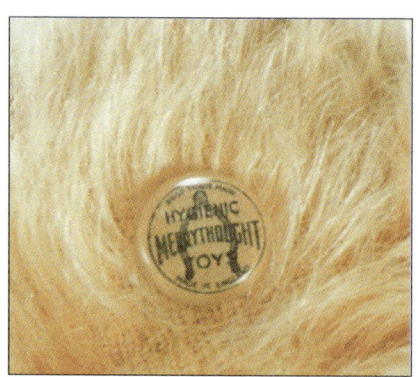

1930s Merrythought Celluloid ear button

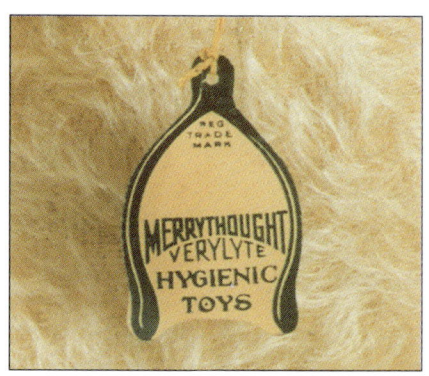

1930s Merrythought chest tag

CHAPTER I

ENGLISH MERRYTHOUGHT TEDDY BEAR
20 inches

Gold mohair; clipped snout; glass eyes; cotton twill paw pads; joined claws on palm pads; kapok stuffed (with excelsior in muzzle area); all jointed; mint; circa 1930.

Marks: Label on foot

Price: $1,400 up

Susan Stanton-Reid Collection

ENGLISH TEDDY BEAR
26 inches

Gold mohair; glass eyes; felt pads; kapok stuffed; all jointed; hard to find a bear with this label; velvet jacket not original to bear; shows wear on stomach area; circa 1930.

Marks: Peacock label on right foot

Price: $1,500 up (without jacket)

ENGLISH PEACOCK TEDDY BEAR
28 inches

Mohair; felt pads; glass eyes; kapok stuffed; all jointed; excellent condition; 1932.

Marks: Label on right foot

Price: $1,500

ENGLISH TEDDY BEAR

21 inches

Pink mohair; glass eyes; velvet pads; kapok stuffed; all jointed; excellent condition; circa 1930.

Marks: None

Price: $950 up

GERMAN JOPI TEDDY BEAR

21 inches

Mohair; felt pads; glass eyes; excelsior stuffed; all jointed; squeeze bellows music box; made by Josef Pitrmann; listed in their 1934 catalogue as *Jackie*; near mint.

Marks: None

Price: $3,500

GERMAN TEDDY BEAR
16 inches
Brown-tipped cream mohair; glass eyes; replaced felt pads; excelsior stuffed; all jointed; near mint; circa 1935.

Marks: None

Price: $650-$700

ENGLISH TEDDY BEAR
30 inches
Gold mohair; glass eyes; velvet pads; excelsior and kapok stuffed; all jointed; made by Chiltern; circa 1935.

Marks: Label on side

Price: $1,250

CHAD VALLEY TEDDY BEAR
22 inches
Gold mohair; glass eyes; felt pads; kapok stuffed; near mint; circa 1935.

Marks: None

Price: $750

ENGLISH CHAD VALLEY TEDDY BEAR
8 inches

Gold mohair; no pads; glass eyes; kapok stuffed; all jointed; excellent condition; circa 1935.

Marks: Metal button on back (unusual placement)

Price: $400-$500

CHILTERN TEDDY BEAR
16 inches

White mohair; glass eyes; velvet pads; excelsior and kapok stuffed; all jointed; near mint; circa 1935.

Marks: None

Price: $825

CHAPTER I

FARNELL TEDDY BEAR

17 inches

Gold mohair; glass eyes; rexine pads (color has flaked off); excelsior and kapok stuffed; all jointed; near mint; circa 1935.

Marks: None

Price: $1,650

FARNELL TEDDY BEAR

22 inches

Dark gold mohair; glass eyes; rexine pads; excelsior and kapok stuffed; all jointed; minor mohair loss; circa 1935.

Marks: None

Price: $1,600

TEDDY BEARS 1902-2000

FARNELL TEDDY BEAR
22 inches
Gold mohair; glass eyes; excelsior and kapok stuffed; rexine pads (flaked off); near mint; circa 1935.

Marks: None

Price: $1,900-$2,000

MERRYTHOUGHT TEDDY BEAR
26 inches
Mohair; glass eyes; replaced pads; excelsior and kapok stuffed; all jointed; circa 1935.

Marks: Label on foot; celluloid button on right ear

Price: $1,650

ENGLISH CHILTERN TEDDY BEAR
19 inches
Pink mohair; felt pads; glass eyes; excelsior and kapok stuffed; all jointed; near mint; circa 1938.

Marks: None

Price: $900-$1,000

CHAPTER I

ENGLISH TEDDY BEAR
18 inches
Gold mohair; felt pads; brown glass eyes; excelsior and kapok stuffed; all jointed; near mint; made by Farnell; late 1930s.

Marks: None

Price: $1,400-$1,500

ENGLISH FARNELL TEDDY BEAR
15 inches
Tan wooly plush; glass eyes; felt pads; kapok stuffed; all jointed; excellent conditions; circa 1938.

Marks: Label on foot; celluloid button on right ear

Price: $450

AMERICAN TEDDY BEAR
17 inches
White mohair; felt pads; glass eyes; excelsior and cotton stuffed; all jointed; mint; circa 1940.

Marks: None

Price: $595

PLUSH TEDDY BEAR

18 inches

Faded pink cotton plush; pinky glass eyes; felt pads; excelsior stuffed; all jointed; circa 1940.

Marks: None

Price: $35-$45

ENGLISH CHAD VALLEY TEDDY BEAR

15 inches

Faded blue mohair; rexine pads; glass eyes; excelsior and kapok stuffed; all jointed; near mint; circa 1940.

Marks: Label on side

Price: $700

AUSTRALIAN BERLEX TEDDY BEAR

Approximately 20 inches

Wearing a scaled-down Australian Diggers uniform and a salesman's sample slouch hat; circa 1940.

Marks: None available

Price: None available

Photo courtesy of and collection of Dot Gillett

CHAPTER I

TEDDY BEAR
15 inches

Tan mohair with inset snout; fabric pads; glass eyes; excelsior stuffed; all jointed; dress not original; manufacturer unknown; circa 1940.

Marks: None

Price: $175-$200

Doris Barrows Collection

JAPANESE TEDDY BEAR
13 inches

Tan wooly plush; orange and black eyes; inset velvet muzzle; excelsior stuffed; velvet pads with swirled airbrushing (bottom cardboard reinforced); all jointed; mouth stitching missing otherwise in excellent condition; possibly made by Kamar Toy Company; circa 1948.

Marks: None

Price: $75-$100

Carmen Lujan Davidson Collection

STEIFF ORIGINAL TEDDY BEAR
3-1/2 inches
Gold mohair; glass eyes; excelsior stuffed; all jointed; mint; 1950s.

Marks: Chest tag
Price: $350-$375

STEIFF TEDDY BEAR
3-1/2 inches
Brown mohair; glass eyes; excelsior stuffed; all jointed; mint; 1950s.

Marks: Script button
Price: $325

STEIFF ORIGINAL TEDDIES
20 inches
Caramel and gold mohair; glass eyes; excelsior stuffed; all jointed; mint; circa 1950s.

Marks: Script button
Price: $1,550 each

CHAPTER 1

STEIFF *ORSI* BEAR
9 inches
Mohair; glass eyes; inset muzzle; open felt mouth; felt pads; swivel head and arms; sitting position; felt bib; mint; circa 1950s.

Marks: Script button
Price: $450 up

STEIFF *ZOTTY* BEAR
8 inches
Mohair; inset muzzle; open felt mouth; felt pads; glass eyes; excelsior stuffed; all jointed; mint; circa 1950s.

Marks: Script button; chest tag
Price: $275

TEDDY BEARS 1902-2000

GERMAN DIEM TEDDY BEAR
16 inches

Mushroom-colored plush; glass eyes; felt pads; excelsior stuffed; all jointed; mint condition; circa 1950.

Marks: None

Price: $350-$375

GERMAN TEDDY BEAR
19 inches

Two-toned mohair in cream with brown tipping; cream inset snout and paw pads (bottom lined with cardboard); clear glass eyes painted on reverse; excelsior stuffed; all jointed; made by Diem; circa 1950.

Marks: None

Price: $650

CHAPTER I

GERMAN DIEM (OF SONNENBERG) TEDDY BEAR

19 inches

Gold mohair; glass eyes; clipped mohair pads; excelsior stuffed; all jointed; mint; circa 1950.

Marks: None

Price: $650 up

GEBR. HERMAN TEDDY BEAR

15 inches

Tan mohair; glass eyes; felt pads; excelsior stuffed; all jointed; near mint; circa 1950.

Marks: None

Price: $475

GERMAN TEDDY BEAR

13 inches

Brown mohair; tan mohair muzzle and feet; open felt mouth; felt nose; glass eyes; soft and hard stuffed; all jointed; plastic collar and bell; circa 1950.

Marks: None

Price: $450

Susan Stanton-Reid Collection

TEDDY BEARS 1902-2000

PLUSH TEDDY BEAR
14 inches
Cotton plush; glass eyes; fabric pads; very firmly stuffed excelsior; all jointed; German; circa 1950.

Marks: None
Price: $90-$125

GERMAN TEDDY BEAR
19 inches
Gold mohair; glass eyes; felt pads; excelsior stuffed; all jointed; excellent condition; circa 1950.

Marks: None
Price: $500-$550

GERMAN TEDDY BEAR
16 inches
Tan mohair; glass eyes; felt pads; excelsior stuffed; all jointed; unusual shaped body; near mint; circa 1950.

Marks: None
Price: $450-$500

EUROPEAN TEDDY BEAR

22 inches

Tan mohair; glass eyes; replaced pads; excelsior stuffed; all jointed; near mint; circa 1950.

Marks: None

Price: $625-$650

SCHUCO YES/NO *TRICKY* MUSICAL TEDDY BEAR

22 inches

Beige mohair; glass eyes; felt pads; excelsior stuffed; all jointed; near mint; circa 1950.

Marks: *Tricky* Tag on chest

Price: Sold at Christie's, London, in 1996 for approximately $3,800.

Photo courtesy of Christie's

AMERICAN TEDDY BEAR

17 inches

Cotton plush; glass eyes; replaced felt pads; excelsior stuffed; all jointed; good condition; romper added; circa 1950.

Marks: None

Price: $150

DEAN'S *TRU-TO-LIFE* TEDDY BEAR

20 inches

Blond mohair; black glass eyes cut into internal rubber face mask; rubber nose, mouth and foot pads with claws; shows overall wear; created by Sylvia Wilgass, designer for Dean's in the 1950s.

Marks: None

Price: Sold at Christie's, London, in 1996 for approximately $1,300.

Photo courtesy of Christie's

ENGLISH CHAD VALLEY TEDDY BEAR

17 inches

Gold mohair; glass eyes; rexine pads; kapok and excelsior stuffed; all jointed; near mint; 1950s.

Marks: Tag on side seam

Price: $600-$625

CHAD VALLEY TEDDY BEAR

17 inches

Gold mohair; glass eyes; felt pads; all jointed; kapok and excelsior stuffed; some staining on pads otherwise mint; 1950s.

Marks: None

Price: $800-$850

CHAD VALLEY *SOOTY* BEAR

15 inches

Gold mohair with black ears; glass eyes; good condition; 1950s.

Marks: Tag under arm

Price: $200-$250

ENGLISH CHAD VALLEY TEDDY BEAR

12 inches

Long gold mohair; glass eyes; rexine pads; excelsior and kapok stuffed; all jointed; wind up music box; near mint; circa 1950.

Marks: None

Price: $950

ENGLISH CHAD VALLEY BEAR

27 inches

Pale gold mohair; glass eyes; rexine pads; excelsior and kapok stuffed; all jointed; mint condition; circa 1950.

Marks: Label sewn on foot and tag in seam

Price: $1,350

CHAPTER I

ENGLISH TEDDY BEAR
36 inches

Gold mohair; glass eyes; velvet pads; excelsior and kapok stuffed; all jointed; near mint; made by Chiltern; circa 1950.

Marks: Tag on side seam

Price: $1,450-$1,500

ENGLISH FARNELL BABY TEDDY BEAR
9 inches

Gold mohair; glass eyes; no foot pads; excelsior stuffed; all jointed; mint; circa 1950.

Marks: None

Price: $425

TEDDY BEARS 1902-2000

ENGLISH CHAD VALLEY TEDDY BEAR

29 inches

Gold mohair; rexine pads; glass eyes; excelsior and kapok stuffed; all jointed; mint; circa 1950.

Marks: Label sewn into front chest; label on foot

Price: $1,150-$1,250

MERRYTHOUGHT *PUNKINHEAD* TEDDY BEAR

16 inches

Brown and gold mohair; white scalp; velvet muzzle; velvet feet; glass eyes; felt shorts; circa 1950s.

Marks: None

Price: $1,200

Photo courtesy of Christie's

CHAPTER 1

IRISH TEDDY BEAR
15 inches

Off-white mohair; glass eyes; rexine pads; excelsior and kapok stuffed; all jointed; mouth is leather covered wood that can be opened and closed by pressing together two amber glass balls that extend from rods at the back of the near; mint; made by Tara; circa 1950.

Marks: None

Price: $795-$825

SCHUCO YES/NO TEDDY BEAR
12 inches

Tan mohair; clear glass eyes; felt pads (bottom replaced); black floss nose, mouth, and claws; excelsior stuffed; worn; clothes not original; 1953.

Marks: None

Price: $400-$450

There are also Schuco Yes/No teddy bears covered in Chapter 5.

GERMAN TEDDY BEAR
12 inches

Tan mohair; clipped inset muzzle; felt pads; glass eyes; excelsior stuffed; all jointed; note two seams in front to the side rather than the usual center body seam; excellent condition; made by Clemens; circa 1955.

Marks: Clemens metal hang tag attached to front

Price: $225-$250

TEDDY BEARS 1902-2000

GERMAN TEDDY BEAR

24 inches

Long shaggy mohair; faded in places from cinnamon to bronze; shaved muzzle; felt pads; replaced eyes (originals were probably larger and glass); excelsior stuffed; pull growler on back (unusual); maker unknown; circa 1955.

Marks: None

Price: $195-$225

MERRYTHOUGHT *CHEEKY* TEDDY BEAR

10 inches

Tan silk plush; velvet muzzle; glass eyes; felt pads; kapok stuffed; all jointed; bell in ear; near mint; circa 1955.

Marks: None

Price: $425

GEBRÜDER HERMAN TEDDY BEAR

20 inches

Gold mohair; glass eyes; felt pads; excelsior stuffed; all jointed; mint; circa 1957.

Marks: None

Price: $675

CHAPTER I

MERRYTHOUGHT *CHEEKY* TEDDY BEAR

19 inches

Gold mohair; velvet muzzle; felt pads; plastic eyes; bell in ear; kapok stuffed; all jointed; mint; 1960s.

Marks: None

Price: $450

MERRYTHOUGHT *CHEEKY* TEDDY BEAR

13-1/2 inches

Gold mohair; felt pads; plastic eyes; velvet muzzle; soft stuffed; all jointed; bells in ears; made by Merrythought, England; circa 1960.

Marks: Label on foot

Price: $350-$400

MERRYTHOUGHT *CHEEKY* TEDDY BEAR

12 inches

Gold mohair; felt pads; glass eyes; velvet muzzle; soft stuffed; all jointed; circa 1960.

Marks: Tag on foot

Price: $425-$450

TEDDY BEARS 1902-2000

ENGLISH MERRYTHOUGHT *CHEEKY* BEAR

25 inches

Gold mohair; velvet muzzle; bells in ear; felt pads; soft stuffed; circa 1960.

Marks: Merrythought tag on foot; extra tag on foot reads "Made in England expressly for Lord and Taylor"

Price: $600 up

ENGLISH MERRYTHOUGHT *POOH*

14 inches

Mohair; twill pads; glass eyes; kapok stuffed; all jointed; mint; circa 1960s.

Marks: Label on foot

Price: $595

TEDDY BEAR SCHOOL
4 inches
Plush bears with pin jointed arms and legs; plastic eyes; originally came in a boxed set with a teacher and desk; made in Japan and issued by Shackman; mint; circa 1960.

Marks: None

Price: $50-$65 as shown

STEIFF TEDDY BEAR
19 inches
Blond mohair; shaved muzzle and eye area; glass eyes; velour pads; excelsior stuffed; all jointed; mint; circa 1965.

Marks: Incised button

Price: $395-$425

STEIFF ORIGINAL TEDDY BEAR
15 inches
Mohair; inserted muzzle area of clipped mohair; glass eyes; felt pads; excelsior stuffed; mint; circa 1965.

Marks: Incised button; chest tag

Price: $450

TEDDY BEARS 1902-2000

SCHUCO TEDDY BEAR
10 inches
Mohair; glass eyes and nose; felt open mouth; soft stuffed; bendable body; Bigo Belo; circa 1965.

Marks: None
Price: $125

MERRYTHOUGHT *CHEEKY* TEDDY BEAR
10 inches
Gold mohair; plastic eyes; kapok stuffed; velvet pads; all jointed; near mint; circa 1965.

Marks: None
Price: $350

GERMAN CLEMENS TEDDY BEAR
22 inches
Mohair; plastic eyes; felt pads; excelsior and soft filling; all jointed; original ribbon; mint; circa 1968.

Marks: Plastic hang tag
Price: $550

CHAPTER I

KNICKERBOCKER TEDDY BEAR

12 inches

Plush; plastic eyes backed by felt; soft stuffed; unjointed; circa 1969.

Marks: "Teddy Kuddle" label sewn into seam

Price: $35

Susan Stanton-Reid Collection

GERMAN TEDDY BEAR

20 inches

Long gold mohair; inset clipped muzzle; glass eyes; open felt mouth; velvet pads; excelsior stuffed; all jointed; original ribbon; made by Fechter; mint; circa 1970.

Marks: Tag on ear

Price: $500 up

Susan Stanton-Reid Collection

ENGLISH DEAN'S TEDDY BEAR

15 inches

Gold mohair; glass eyes; suedene pads; soft stuffed; all jointed; mint; circa 1970.

Marks: Dean's tag sewn in seam

Price: $350-$375

MERRYTHOUGHT *CHEEKY* TEDDY BEAR

16 inches

Plush; plastic eyes; kapok stuffed; all jointed; mint; circa 1970s.

Marks: All tags/labels

Price: $325

CHAPTER I

TOYLAND TEDDY BEAR
24 inches
Brown plush; peach inset plush muzzle and paw pads; plastic eyes and nose; poly filled; all jointed; made in Israel; circa 1975.

Marks: Label sewn in side seam
Price: $50-$75
Susan Stanton-Reid Collection

GERMAN GRISLY TEDDY BEAR
15 inches
Blond mohair; brown clipped mohair muzzle, inner ears and foot pads; plastic eyes; excelsior stuffed; all jointed; mint; circa 1980.

Marks: Paper hang tag
Price: $100-$150
Susan Stanton-Reid Collection

VELVET TEDDY BEAR
9 inches
Made by Clancey Collecibles, England; gold velour; felt eyes and nose; jointed at limbs by thread; soft stuffed; mint; 1980s.

Marks: paper hang tag
Price: $25-$35

NISBET "HARRODS" TEDDY BEAR
15 inches
Bully bear (named after Peter Bull, English actor and father of the teddy bear movement); made especially for Harrods Department Store, London; wearing the store's doorman's hat; gold mohair; plastic eyes; velvet pads; 1980s.

Marks: Label sewn on foot pad
Price: $175-$200

CHINESE TEDDY BEARS
8 inches and 11 inches
Plush; made in China for mass marketing; 1980s.

Marks: Seam tags
Price: $25-$45

STEIFF TEDDY BEAR

12 inches

Mohair; made especially for the opening of the Margaret Strong Museum in Rochester, NY; 1982.

Marks: Brass button; hang tag; signed on foot by Han Otto Steiff

Price: $450

GEBR. HERMANN *ZOTTY* BEAR

16 inches

Tipped mohair; glass eyes; excelsior stuffed; all jointed; 1983.

Marks: Plastic hang tag; paper hang tag

Price: $325

GEBR. HERMANN *ZOTTY* TEDDY BEAR

20 inches

Tipped mohair; plastic eyes; excelsior and soft stuffed; all jointed; 1983.

Marks: Plastic hang tag; paper hang tag

Price: $425

GEBR. HERMANN TEDDY BEAR

13 inches

Mohair; plastic eyes; excelsior stuffed; straw hat; all jointed; wind up music box plays "The Teddy Bear's Picnic;" 1984.

Marks: Plastic hang tag; paper hang tag sewn-in label

Price: $325

HELEN SIEVERLING TEDDY BEAR

12 inches

Mohair; leather pads; all jointed; made by Gebr. Hermann to honor Helen Sieverling, writer for *Teddy Bear and Friends* magazine; M.I.B. 1985.

Marks: Four hang tags; signed on foot

Price: $175 up

STEIFF GIENGEN TEDDY BEAR

15 inches

Mohair; replica of a bear produced in 1906; one of four sizes; circa 1985.

Marks: Brass button; Unicorn (symbol of Giengen) chest tag

Price: $500

DAKIN 30TH ANNIVERSARY TEDDY BEAR

14 inches

White plush; plastic eyes; all jointed; 1985.

Marks: Metal hang tag with "Dakin 30 Years;" seam tag

Price: $150

DAKIN *ELEGANTE*

16 inches

Plush; plastic eyes; all jointed; wear spectacles; plaid bow; 1983.

Marks: Leather hang tag; seam tag

Price: $85

ENGLISH TEDDY BEAR

24 inches

Brown plush; plastic eyes; kapok stuffed; all jointed; made by Alresford; 1983.

Marks: None

Price: $125

ENGLISH TEDDY BEAR

20 inches

Gray plush; plastic eyes; soft stuffed; unjointed; made by Alresford; 1983.

Marks: Paper hang tag; sewn on label

Price: $60

CHAPTER I

ENGLISH MERRYTHOUGHT TEDDY BEAR

13 inches

Gold mohair; plastic eyes; felt pads; soft stuffed; all jointed; green knit scarf with wishbone; mint; 1984.

Marks: Label on foot; hang tag

Price: $225-$250

PAT SCHOONMAKER TEDDY BEAR

15 inches

Tri-colored mohair in jester fashion; made by Dean's, England, to honor Pat Schoonmaker, author of one of the first comprehensive Teddy Books; M.I.B.; circa 1985.

Marks: Paper hang tags

Price: $325

STEIFF TEDDY CLOWN

12 inches

Replica made in 1986 emulating the clown bear of the 1930s.

Marks: Brass button; chest tag

Price: $350 up

SMITHSONIAN TEDDY BEAR

24 inches

Plush; replica of the first Ideal Bear; manufactured by Determined Productions Inc. ©1987 Smithsonian Institution.

Marks: Seam tag; hang tag

Price: $325

CHAPTER I

GUND TEDDY BEAR
15 inches
Brown plush; velvet pads; made for B. Altman Stores by Gund in 1987.
Marks: Label on foot; tag on back seam
Price: $95-$100

ROBERT RAIKES TEDDY BEAR
11 inches
Plush; wooden face; dressed as an Angel with wings; made by Applause; ©1989.

Marks: Seam tag; hang tag
Price: $200

HARROD'S TEDDY BEAR
12 inches
Plush; glass eyes; felt pads; soft stuffed; all jointed; made in China for Harrod's Department Store in London; mint; 1990s.

Marks: Label in seam; hang tag on ear
Price: $25

GUND *AUNT ELDERBERRY AND DEWDROP*

17 inches and 6 inches

White plush; leather pads; plastic eyes; all jointed; neck bows; hat on baby; limited edition of 1,250; 1991.

Marks: Seam tags; neck tags; signed on foot

Price: $195

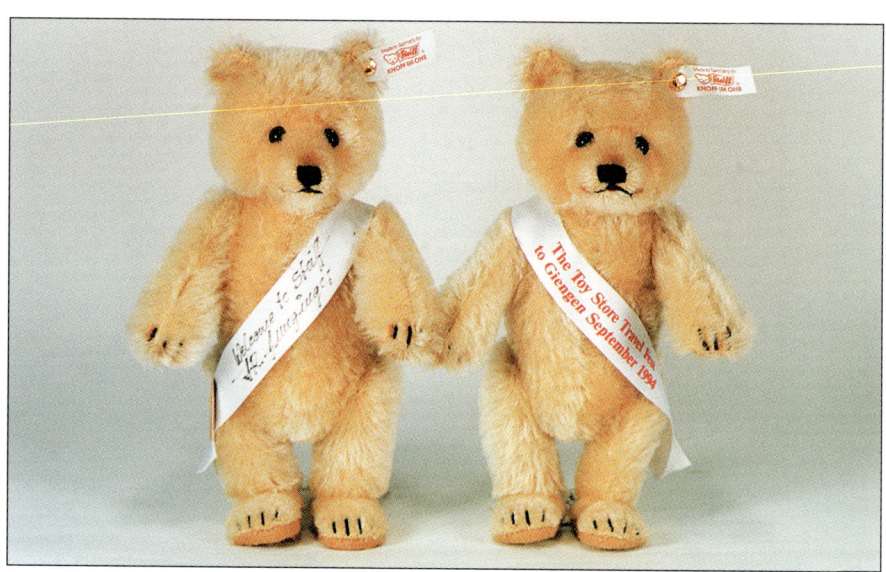

STEIFF TEDDY BABIES

9 inches

Specialty bears assembled for the Toy Store's (of Toledo, Ohio) trip to Germany in 1994; only 12 worldwide.

Marks: Ribbon banners commemorating the event; brass buttons

Price: $1,000

CHAPTER I

VERMONT TEDDY BEAR
15 inches
Plush; plastic eyes; all jointed; cotton dress; in box; mint; 1992.

Marks: Hang tag; seam tag
Price: $195

VALENTINO THE BEAR
White plush with red heart; birthday February 14, 1994.

Marks: Tush tag; label in ear

SAM TEDDY BEAR
16 inches
Cinnamon plush; plush pads; plastic eyes; unjointed; soft stuffed; designed by Sally Winey for Ty Inc.; 1995.

Marks: Hang tag; signed by Sally on foot.
Price: $25-$30

TEDDY BEARS 1902-2000

STEIFF BOXED SET
15 inches
Satin lined wooden box holding a book on Steiff Bears by the Cieslik's and two teddies; Limited to 1,000.

Price: $700

PEACE THE BEAR
Multi-tie-dyed plush with Olympic insignia; birthday February 1, 1996.

Marks: Tush tag; label in ear

CHAPTER I

CURLY THE BEAR
Tan plush with ribbon only; birthday April 12, 1996

Marks: Tush tag; label in ear

MAPLE THE BEAR
Available only in Canada; white plush with Canadian flag; birthday July 1, 1996.

Marks: Tush tag; label in ear

PRINCESS THE BEAR
Purple plush with embroidered white rose; born in 1997; all profits donated to the Princess of Wales Memorial Fund.

Marks: Tush tag; label in ear

STEIFF JUBILEE BEAR

12 inches

Brown mohair (one of three colors); glass eyes; felt pads; all jointed; made to commemorate Margarete Steiff's 150th birthday in 1997.

Marks: Brass buttons; ceramic disk on ribbon

Price: $200

STEIFF GIENGEN FESTIVAL BEARS

13 inches

Blue-eyed bears made for the conventions in Germany.

Marks: Brass button; label in ear; hang tags

Blackey (1997): $750 up; Whitey (1998): $595 up; Rosey (1999): $595 up

CHAPTER I

MILLENNIUM 2000

Embroidered world logo on chest; birthday January 1, 1999.

Marks: Tush tag; label in ear

STEIFF HELLO GOODBYE SET

8-3/4 inches

Limited edition set open until the end of the year 2000.

Price: $450

FRANK

11 inches

Replica of the bear that was on the 1998 U.S. postage stamp; limited edition of 2,000; 1999/2000; in presentation box.

Marks: Tag in seam

Price: $149

STEIFF HUCKLEBERRY FINN TEDDY BEAR

11-1/2 inches

Limited edition of 1,500 pieces for the North American market; 2001.

Price: $275

SMITHSONIAN CENTENNIAL TEDDY BEAR

26 inches

On the 60th anniversary of Teddy's birth, Benjamin Michtom, son of Ideal Toy Company's founder, presented Theodore Roosevelt's grandson Kermit with an early Ideal teddy bear. Honoring Michtom's intent, this bear was donated to the Smithsonian in 1964 and became part of the collections at the National Museum of American History. In honor of the Teddy's 100th birthday, the museum commissioned Hermann-Spielwaren of Germany to duplicate this early example.

Marks: Hang tag; label

Price: $275

RE-ISSUES, CLUB BEAR AND LIMITED EDITIONS • CHAPTER II

When the teddy bear became such an important hobby, and the craving for the earliest examples sometimes exceeded the supply, insightful companies started to re-issue examples based on designs from previous eras. Many of these are offered in limited editions with certificates and presentation boxes.

Collectibles also include special products for a specific store or event and also those models made only for a limited period of time.

Steiff also originated a club where, members only, could purchase a special bear (or animal) just for them. Other companies followed suit and now clubs are a viable movement in the collection arena.

STEIFF *RICHARD STEIFF* BEAR

12 inches
Gray mohair, replica of 1983. Mint in presentation box.

Marks: Brass button; white replica ear tag; hang tag (missing on this one)

Price: $475

RE-ISSUES, CLUB BEAR AND LIMITED EDITIONS

MERRYTHOUGHT DIAMOND JUBILEE BEAR

15 inches

Made in limited edition of 1,000 for Harrod's Department Store; mohair; plastic eyes; all jointed; M.I.B.; 1983.

Marks: Label on foot; label on side seams; hang tag

Price: $275

MERRYTHOUGHT ANNIVERSARY TEDDY BEAR

10 inches

Gold mohair; plastic eyes; soft stuffed; commemorates the Statue of Liberty's 100th birthday; mint; 1986.

Marks: Labels sewn into seam and across the foot

Price: $150-$175

STEIFF FAO SCHWARZ TEDDY BEAR

12 inches

Mohair; made for the store's 125th Anniversary in 1987; limited edition of 1,000; presentation box.

Marks: Brass button: FAO hang tag

Price: $350

GEBR. HERMANN BERLIN WALL TEDDY BEAR

11 inches

Mohair; plastic eyes; firmly stuffed; all jointed; wears a collar; carries a bag with an actual piece of the wall that was torn down; Limited edition of 2,000; 1989.

Marks: Plastic and paper hang tags

Price: $395

STEIFF TEDDY *BABY ROSE*

7 inches

Mohair; made for Hobby Center Toys (now The Toy Store) in Toledo, Ohio. Mint; 1990

Marks: All buttons, labels and tags

Price: $450 up

RE-ISSUES, CLUB BEAR AND LIMITED EDITIONS

UFDC LUNCHEON TEDDY BEAR

9 inches

Made by Bearly There Inc. in 1990 for the Washington D.C. Convention; signed by Linda Spiegel Lohre and wears a paper patriotic banner.

Marks: Hang tag; label on back seam

Price: $90-$110

Donna Felger Collection

UFDC LUNCHEON TEDDY BEAR

10 inches

Francois by artist Kathi Clark; produced for the convention held in New Orleans, LA in 1991; limited edition of 400.

Marks: Hang tag signed by the artist

Price: $100-$125

Donna Felger Collection

CHAPTER 11

STEIFF CONVENTION TEDDY BEAR

24 inches

Gold mohair; made especially for the 2nd Disneyland Convention in 1993; music box plays "When You Wish Upon a Star" and "It's a Small World"; limited edition of 25.

Marks: Brass button; hang tags; ribbon with logo; two convention buttons

Price: $5,000

UFDC LUNCHEON TEDDY BEAR REGINA

7 inches

Made for the 1994 convention in Atlanta, GA. Mohair bear with sachet and presentation box; designed by John Axe and manufactured by Alpha Farnell in a limited edition of 313. Oliver Holmes, Chairman of the Merrythought Company in England registered the Farnell name in the 1990s. He is therefore able to use this company's name on selected products.

Marks: Label on box with historical data; label sewn into side seam

Price: $75-$100

Donna Felger Collection

RE-ISSUES, CLUB BEAR AND LIMITED EDITIONS

GEBR. HERMANN TEDDY BEAR
8 inches

Mohair; all jointed; limited edition of 1,000; 1994.

Marks: Plastic hang tag; paper hang tag and certificate

Price: $75-$90

GEBR. HERMANN GERMAN "MUSEUM" TEDDY BEAR
12 inches

Made in a limited edition of 100 pieces for the Doll and Toy Museum in Rothenbrug, Germany in 1994; data embroidered on felt apron; with certificate.

Marks: Label in seam; button on back of head; plastic hang tag

Price: $225

ENGLISH GABRIELLE
PADDINGTON BEAR
13 inches

Mohair; plastic eyes; well-made felt toggle coat and hat; vinyl Wellington's; carries suitcase; limited edition of 5,000; beautiful presentation box; labels and hang tags; M.I.B.; 1995.

Marks: As stated

Price: $325 up

ENGLISH GABRIELLE *AUNT LUCY*
14 inches

Paddington's Aunt is made of mohair, wears glasses and is beautifully dressed in Peruvian clothes; she is presented in a beautiful and imaginative box; limited edition of 2,000; M.I.B.; 1995.

Marks: Labels and hang tags

Price: $325 up

HONG KONG CLUB TEDDY BEAR
13 inches

Mohair; plastic eyes; felt paw pads; all jointed; made by Merrythought for the Animal Kingdom Shop in Hong Kong; 1996.

Marks: Label; hang tag; ribbon and felt Club Bear emblem

Price: $165

R. JOHN WRIGHT TEDDY BEAR
9 inches

Wooly fabric; glass googly eyes, felt pads; all jointed; red ribbon adorned with Wright's logo pin. First Teddy (other than Pooh); limited edition for 1998 club members. Mint in box with certificate.

Price: $425 at issue

PRINCE ALBERT TEDDY BEAR
16 inches

Mohair bear wearing a blue velvet cloak; all jointed; made by Hermann Spielwaren Gamb H to commemorate Queen Victoria's consort's German birth in Coburg; mint; 1990s.

Marks: Embroidered on foot; hang tags

Price: $200-$225

Maria Bluni Collection

FRANK REPLICA
10 inches

A replica of the stamp bear first issued in late 1999; mohair; embroidered pads; patriotic banner; hang tag; presentation box. Shown here with original (left) Ideal teddy bear.

Price: $149 at issue

ARTIST BEARS • CHAPTER III

While the term "Artist Bears" has been recognized for just over 20 years, it is now a very popular collecting area in the teddy bear world. Although the movement had its genesis in the United States, there are now extremely talented artists world-wide.

The mother of the artist bear movement is the enormously talented Beverly Port. Beverly pioneered for the evolution of bear making into an art form and consistently promotes those artists who came after her. I have included some of her early works and a sampling of what other creative people have accomplished.

ARTIST TEDDY BEAR
16 inches

Blue Boy made by Beverly Port; plush forms jester suit; trimmed in crochet lace; 1984.

Marks: Hanging silver medallion

Price: $395

ARTIST JESTER BEAR

16 inches

Alpaca in made-on jester suit; a "Time Machine Teddy" by Beverly Port; carries a rattle and resin teddy head on a stick; wind up music box; 1984.

Marks: Hanging silver medallion

Price: $750

SCHOOLBOY

17 inches

Mohair; detailed costuming; by artist Gary Nett; 1980s.

Marks: Stamped on body front

Price: $395

BEN FRANKLIN

19 inches

By artist Gary Nett; beautiful and detailed costume; 1980s.

Marks: Information on kite

Price: $395

WENDY BRENT TEDDY BEARS
24 and 20 inches
Special edition bears; Angel and Christmas themes; "Noses of Roses" molded muzzles that incorporate a scent; glass eyes; trapunto needlework paw pads; 1980s.
Price: $350-$450 each

POOH-TYPE BEAR
11 inches
Plush; made by Flora Mediate; 1983.

Marks: Sewn label on back
Price: $100

ARTIST TEDDY BEAR
13-1/2 inches

The Muffin Man; mohair; glass eyes; all jointed; dressed in wool costume; carries a wooden tray of breads on his head; made by Nancy Crowe; 1988.

Marks: Hang tag

Price: $350

ARTIST TEDDY BEAR
12 inches

The Nanny; mohair; glass eyes; all jointed; beautifully dressed and accessorized; made by Nancy Crowe; 1988.

Marks: Hang tag

Price: $325

LASTING ENDEARMENT TEDDY BEAR

21 inches

Count Alexi Bearinski; limited edition of 200 in the 1980s; plush is applied to stationary form; glass eyes; beautifully dressed; mint.

Marks: Booklet and attached tag

Price: $800 up

LASTING ENDEARMENT TEDDY BEARS

21 inches and 10 inches

Sonja Grizzlyann Bearinski and Baby Noel; plush applied over form; glass eyes; open mouth with tongue; artistically dressed and carry sequined ice skates; Baby Noel is a traditionally jointed teddy bear and comes in a sled; mint; 1980s.

Marks: Tagged and booklet

Price: $800 up

ARTIST BEARS

JESTER ON A STICK
16 inches overal

Mohair head with lace trimmed hat and ruff; by Kathy Myers; 1980s.

Marks: Seam tag

Price: $80

MINI TEDDY BEARS
Panda: 2-1/4 inches; Teddy: 3 inches

Panda is made of mini mohair; neck trim; by Kelli Kirby; 1998. *Teddy* is made of mini mohair; neck ribbon; by Dickie Harrison; 1980s.

Panda Marks: Hang tag

Teddy Marks: Hang tag on back

Price: Panda: $95; Teddy: $125

MISS MADISON
20 inches

Mohair; one-of-a-kind special order; by Ronwyn Graham; 1998.

Price: $350

WOOLEY TEDDY BEAR

12 inches

Alpaca bear with antique shoe button eyes and vintage ornament. Presented to Chris Revi, editor of *Teddy Bear Review* in 1992 by artist Pamela Wooley.

Marks: Hang tag

Price: $250

ARTIST TEDDY BEAR

22 inches

Made from an antique sleigh blanket; shoe button eyes; painted canvas feet; by Canadian artist Donna McPherson; 1995

Marks: None

Price: $250

SLEIGH TEDDY BEAR

22 inches

Made from an antique sleigh blanket and old shoe buttons for eyes; vintage pads and trim; by Donna McPherson; 1990s.

Marks: Hang tag

Price: $350

HUGGY TEDDY BEAR
17 inches

Mohair; glass eyes; dressed in vintage clothing by Canadian artist Donna McPherson; 1990s.

Marks: Hang tag

Price: $450

ARTIST TEDDY BEAR
24 inches

Barefoot teddy *Mary Ann* by artist Gloria Franks; dressed and carrying a rag doll; 1996.

Price: $450 up

CHAPTER III

MINI TEDDY BEARS

Bear Head Brooch in Mad Hatter's Hat: Artist unknown; 1990s.
Fur dressed bear: 3 inches by Mary Ann Gebhardt; 1997;
Bear in bib: 2 inches by Debbie Kesling; 1992;

Price: Brooch: $95; Fur Dressed: $215; Bear in Bib: $165

BASKET OF TEDDY BEARS

16 inches

Mohair selection in various colors; by Ronwyn Graham; 1997.

Price: $225 each

ARTIST BEARS

LARRABEE
21 inches
Mohair; wearing collar and tie; by Ronwyn Graham; 1997.
Price: $327

WINSTON
28 inches
Mohair; wearing collar and tie; by Ronwyn Graham: 1997.
Price: $450

PERRI
22 inches
Mohair; wearing jabot and tie; 1998; by Australian artist Ronwyn Graham.
Price: $380

BELLE
20 inches
Mohair; wearing lace collar; 1998; by Australian artist Ronwyn Graham.
Price: $380

NOVELTY BEARS AND ANIMALS • CHAPTER IV

The teddies and animals that fall into this category present a wide and varied selection. They run the gamut in aesthetics as well as price. A perfectly executed Schuco compact bear with its ingenious engineering or a muff with an attached head, arms and legs can surely be considered innovative. There are also teddies that can be purchased for about $20 (sometimes even less) and these too, can be considered novelties. The choice can be awe-inspiring or just plain fun.

AMERICAN TEDDY DOLL
14 inches

Mohair; glass eyes; felt pads; excelsior stuffed; all jointed; celluloid head under chin; made by Baker and Bigler; mint; circa 1907.

Marks: None

Price: $3,000

Close up of Baker of and Bigler Teddy Doll showing the insertion of the doll's head.

NOVELTY BEARS AND ANIMALS

ELECTRIC EYE TEDDY BEAR
20 inches

Gold mohair; felt pads; excelsior stuffed; one light bulb and battery pack missing; circa 1907.

Marks: None

Price: $350

AMERICAN ELECTRIC EYE TEDDY BEAR
22 inches

Red mohair; felt pads; swivel arms; glass eyes replace original light bulbs; excelsior stuffed; battery pack removed; circa 1907.

Marks: None

Price: $300-$325

AMERICAN TEDDY DOLL
11 inches

Bisque doll head; mohair body and hood; swivel limbs; near mint; circa 1910.

Marks: None

Price: $300-$350

TEDDY BEAR PURSE

9 inches

Gold mohair; shoe button eyes; felt pads; all jointed; body forms purse; slight wear; circa 1910.

Marks: None

Price: Approximately $1,700 at Christie's, London, auction in 1999.

Photo courtesy of Christie's

TEDDY RAG SHEET

14 inches when assembled

Cotton sheet with front and back of teddy bear; to be cut, sewn and stuffed by the home-sewer; English; circa 1918.

Marks: Printed "Teddy" on back of head; also "British Made Reg'd" on back of legs

Price: $125

MUSICAL JOPI TEDDY BEAR

15 inches

Orange tipped cream mohair; glass eyes; felt pads (3 recovered); excelsior stuffed; all jointed; original bell; music box is operated by squeezing tummy; circa 1920.

Marks: None

Price: Sold at Christie's, London, auction in 1996 for approximately $3,700.

Photo courtesy of Christie's

BEAVER FUR MUFF IN ORIGINAL BOX

Box is cylindrical in shape and has nice logo of a bear; from a shop in Stuttgart, Germany; 1920s.

Marks: On box

Price: $295

PUSS IN BOOTS DOLL

14 inches

Gold mohair; felt face; shoe button eyes; made-on felt shoes; jointed limbs; near mint; circa 1920; maker unknown.

Marks: None

Price: $495-$525

BEAR BRAND TEDDY BEAR

10 inches

Cloth lithograph; along with a Bear Brand puzzle to assemble; circa 1920.

Marks: *Benny Bear* on bear's reverse side; logos on puzzle envelope

Price: $265

NOVELTY BEARS AND ANIMALS

SCHUCO PERFUME BEAR
2-1/2 inches

Pale orange mohair; bead eyes; metal armature; jointed limbs; head lifts off to reveal scent bottle; near mint; circa 1920.

Marks: None

Price: $750 up

SCHUCO MONKEY FLASK
8 inches

Faded lavender mohair over metal: felt paws; clay-like molded face; head lifts off to reveal flask; good condition; circa 1920.

Marks: None

Price: $895

CAT ATOMIZER
2-1/2 inches

Black velvet and pipe cleaner tail and ears; glass eyes; perfume is poured into brass covered opening on bottom; when body is pressed, scent comes out of cat's nose; probably Schuco; 1920s.

Marks: German data engraved on brass button

Price: $650

SCHUCO DWARF PERFUME BOTTLE

5 inches

Felt over metal; clay-like face; mohair hat; head lifts off to reveal perfume bottle; excellent condition; circa 1920.

Marks: None

Price: $895

SCHUCO ATOMIZER BEAR

3 inches

Mohair; bead eyes; fill from bottom; press stomach and scent comes out of nose; near mint; circa 1920.

Marks: None

Price: $1,150

GERMAN MUSICAL CRÄMER TEDDY BEAR

17 inches

Peachy mohair; glass eyes; felt pads; excelsior stuffed; music activates by moving head back and forth; near mint; rare, 1925.

Marks: None

Price: $4,500

SCHUCO PERFUME TEDDY BEAR

5 inches

Gold mohair over metal; black metal bead eyes; metal glasses; head lifts off to reveal perfume bottle; jointed limbs; near mint; circa 1925.

Marks: None

Price: $850

SCHUCO PERFUME RABBIT

5 inches

Tan mohair (some wear); metal aramature; jointed limbs; head lifts off to reveal scent bottle; red faceted "jewel" eyes (available only by special order); circa 1925.

Marks: None

Price: $775

SCHUCO PERFUME BELLHOP MONKEY

5 inches

Mohair head; clay-like metal face; felt pads and clothes over metal that form body; head lifts off to reveal perfume bottle; jointed limbs; near mint; circa 1925.

Marks: None

Price: $550-$575

SCHUCO COMPACT TEDDY
3-1/2 inches

Gold mohair over metal; bead eyes; all jointed; stomach opens to reveal compact (puff missing); head lifts off to reveal lipstick (case missing); shows wear; circa 1925.

Marks: None

Price: $600-$650

PETER TEDDY BEAR
14 inches

Brown and white mohair; felt pads; wooden eyes that roll with tongue when head is moved; papier machÈ head; composition nose and open mouth; body excelsior; all jointed; original ribbon; M.I.B. circa 1925; Gebr. Sussenguth.

Marks: Chest tag *"Peter"/Ges./NR 895257*; box with label

Price: $3,500 up

Lorraine Oakley Collection

SCHUCO SPANIEL COMPACT
3 inches

Velvet and mohair; glass eyes;
opens to reveal mirror; powder puff missing; inscribed on the inside that it was made by Schuco in Germany and patented May 18, 1926; near mint.

Marks: Inscribed inside
Pat'd May 18, 1926
USA Nov. 27, 1928
Eng. Pat 286727
Schuco/Erevete' France SEDE
D R Patents/Made in Germany

Price: $1,700

SCHUCO DOG FACE COMPACT
3-3/4 inches

Tan velvet face with airbrushed muzzle and wrinkles; rust velvet ears; glass googly eyes backed with felt; felt tongue; brass interior to hold powder; excellent condition; 1926. (*Note: There is also a cat compact with the body as in dog's face and the head and tail placed approximately where the dog's ears are.*)

Marks: Inscribed inside
Pat'd May 18, 1926
USA Nov. 27, 1928
Eng. Pat 286727
Schuco/Erevete' France SEDE
D R Patents/Made in Germany

Price: $1,450-$1,500

Katie Mooney Collection

EMBROIDERED TEDDY BEAR
13 inches

Sewn from what appears to be a commercial product; bear is on dyed linen fabric; sewn, embroidered and assembled; soft stuffed; possibly from a Three Bears set; excellent condition; 1930s.

Marks: None

Price: $60-$75

SCHUCO *JOE* YO YO

6 inches

Metal with pipe cleaner legs; felt paws; mint; 1932.

Marks: None

Price: $2,000

GERMAN PETZ PULL TOY

6 inches

Bears are yellow silky plush; glass eyes; original ribbons; the first Teddy's paws are fixed to the handle bars and feet fixed to the pedals on the blue tricycle; red wooden wheels; circa 1935.

Marks: Porcelain chest buttons

Price: Sold at Christie's, London, in 1996 for approximately $1,700.

Photo courtesy of Christie's

SCHUCO TWO-FACED *JANUS* TEDDY BEAR
3-1/2 inches

Cinnamon mohair; metal armature; bead eyes on the teddy bead; turn knob on bottom and the head swivels to a Golliwogg type face with googly eyes and mouth; all jointed; near mint; 1950s.

Marks: None

Price: $1,200

SCHUCO PERFUME BOTTLE BEAR
5 inches

Gold mohair over metal; metal eyes; jointed legs and arms; head lifts off to reveal glass perfume vial; circa 1950.

Marks: None

Price: $450 up

CHAPTER IV

ADVERTISING SET

Plush bear and clock advertising Snow Crop orange juice; the bear's eyes on the clock move back and forth as the pendulum swings; circa 1950.

Price: $550

SMOKEY BEAR
18 inches

Brown plush; molded vinyl head, hands and feet; painted mouth and shadings; glassene eyes; retains original pants with belt, hat and badge; made by Ideal; the first version; near mint; 1953.

Marks: Incised data on back of the head

Price: $200 up

SMOKEY THE BEAR
16 inches

Rust plush; rubber molded face; made-on cotton pants; retains belt and badge; made by Ideal; near mint; 1954.

Marks: Label in seam

Price: $185-$200

KNICKERBOCKER *POUTING ANIMALS* BEARS

7 inches and 13 inches

Brown plush; vinyl faces; soft stuffed; non-jointed; near mint; 1950s.

Marks: Tags sewn in leg seam

Price: $25-$60

GRISLY DOG PURSE

7 inches

Mohair; glass eyes; excelsior head and limbs; purse forms the body; shows wear; 1950s.

Marks: None

Price: $100

ENGLISH MERRYTHOUGHT *CHEEKY* MUFF

12 inches

Mohair head and legs; velvet muzzle; plastic eyes; felt foot pads; plush body forms muff that is lined in pink silky fabric; near mint; 1960s.

Marks: Label sewn on side

Price: $375

CHAPTER IV

TEDDY EDWARD
13 inches

Gold mohair; black glass eyes; velvet pads; all jointed. This bear was the protagonist in a series of books and films by the late Patrick Mathews. He was photographed all over the world in natural poses and frequently with other animals. He was sold with all the copyrights and various other animals, films, magazines and assorted memorabilia. Sold at Christie's Auction House in London in December 1996. Purchased by Yoshi Sekiguchi, owner of two Japanese museums.

Price: Approximately $60,000

Photo courtesy of Christie's

NOVELTY BEARS AND ANIMALS

POOH NIGHTDRESS CASE
14 inches

Mohair head, paws and feet attached to a velvet and satin zippered case to hold nightwear. *Pooh* painted on pillow; made by Merrythought in the 1960s; original owner was Colonel T.R. Henderson, the man behind England's chapter of Good Bears of the World.

Marks: Hang tag

Price: $1,100 up

STEIFF HIDE-A-GIFTS
5 inches

Mohair dog; plush bear; felt clothes; hollow underneath to hide small gifts for children; mint; circa 1965.

Marks: Incised buttons; chest tag

Price: $175 each

MISHA OLYMPIC BEAR
18 inches

Brown and white plush; felt eyes; soft stuffed; made for the 1980 Olympics in Moscow; Olympic rings and ribbon colors at the waist; mint; hard to find with all tags complete.

Marks: Cloth R. Dakin Co. tag; paper tag in ear

Price: $85-$95

CHAPTER IV

ANXIETY BEAR

This plush bear is encased in a 11 x 7 x 5-1/2 inch metal box; hammer attached by chain; Bond's Bear by Nistar Ltd. 1985; boxed.

Marks: All data imprinted on box

Price: $225

TOUGH TED NOVELTY BEAR

7 inches sitting

Plus Teddy sitting in a presentation box; anchor "tattoo" on left arm; crumpled ear; made in China; bought at Hamleys Toy Store, London; 1985.

Marks: Data on box; Golden Bear Products Ltd.

Price: $45-$50

Donna Felger Collection

HARLEY DAVIDSON BEAR

17 inches

Plush; dressed; novelty bear; 1990s

Marks: Various logos and hang tag

Price: Gift to author

STEIFF *DONALD* BEAR

14 inches

White mohair with duck bill airbrushed gold; dressed like Donald Duck; made for 1993 convention at Disney World; ©Disney Enterprises, ltd. Edition of 1,500.

Marks: Brass button; white stock tag; hang tag on sandal

PATTI PLATYPUS

Bright pink and gold plush; birthday January 6, 1993.

Marks: Ty hang tag; label

MYSTIC UNICORN

White Plush; iridescent horn; birthday May 21, 1994.

Marks: Ty hang tag; label

MECHANICAL BEARS AND ANIMALS • CHAPTER V

The Bing Company, of Germany, led the field in the early days when it came to mechanical wonders. Teddy bears with heads that moved back and forth, rabbits that rotated around eggs and leaping frogs are just a few of the novelties produced by this firm. Schuco, also a German company, followed suit. Their most well-known and idolized toys are the Yes/No variety that were introduced in the 1920s and continued well after WW II. Other companies, including Steiff, also designed interesting and innovative designs.

MECHANICAL GERMAN TEDDY BEAR

12 inches

Gold mohair; replaced felt pads; shoe button eyes; excelsior stuffed; all jointed; key wind on right side causes head to move back and forth; excellent condition; made by Bing; circa 1908.

Marks: Button on left side

Price: $3,500-$4,000

BING MECHANICAL RABBIT

6 inches (including ears)

Mohair; glass eyes; on wheels; by winding the key the ball rotates and rabbit "dances;" mint; circa 1913.

Marks: None

Price: $2,300

SCHUCO MECHANICAL TEDDY BEAR

10 inches

Gold mohair; shoe button eyes; made-on red coat; missing hat; key wound; walks backward and forward and circles to the right and left; excellent condition; circa 1920.

Marks: None

Price: $2,500

CHAPTER V

BING KEY WIND LEAPING FROG
7 inches (plus pole)
Green and yellow felt; canvas hat; metal pole; glass eyes; excelsior stuffed; circa 1920.
Marks: Metal B W (Bing Werke) tag on arm
Price: $850 up when operating

SCHUCO YES/NO MONKEY
16 inches
Gold mohair; felt face and paws; inset glass eyes; excelsior stuffed; all jointed; wears glasses; near mint; rare; circa 1920.

Marks: None
Price: $1,195

SCHUCO MECHANICAL TEDDY BEAR

5 inches

Gold mohair over metal; black metal eyes; swivel head and arms; red felt pants and tasseled hat; dances when key wound; excellent condition; circa 1925.

Marks: None

Price: $650-$700

SCHUCO PERFUME TEDDY BEAR

5 inches

Gold mohair over metal; black metal eyes; jointed limbs; head lifts off to reveal glass perfume bottle; excellent condition; circa 1925.

Marks: None

Price: $450-$600

STEIFF CAT

9 inches

Mohair; glass eyes; all jointed; tail turns head; mint; circa 1930.

Marks: Printed FF button

Price: $2,500

CHAPTER V

SCHUCO DANCING CLOWN
4-1/2 inches

Metal with felt clothes; when he dances, the ball twirls around; circa 1948.

Marks: On foot. US Zone/Schuco/Made in Germany

Price: $425-$450

MECHANICAL RABBITS
6 inches (plus ears)

Plush over machè; felt and cotton clothes; key wound dancers; made in Germany; mint; circa 1949.

Marks: U S Zone paper label on foot

Price: $400-$450 pair

SCHUCO TUMBLING MOUSE
4 inches

Felt over metal; key wound acrobatic; replaced key; in working condition; circa 1950

Marks: Stamped on base "Schuco-Patent-Turn"

"Made in U S Zone/Germany"

Price: $195-$200

SCHUCO YES/NO ELEPHANT
8 inches

Gray mohair; pink mohair pads; glass googly eyes; open red felt mouth; all jointed; hard and soft stuffed; mint; circa 1950.

Marks: None

Price: $800 up

SCHUCO YES/NO TEDDY BEAR
5 inches

Gold mohair; glass eyes; all jointed; red felt tongue; "Berlin" banner across chest; metal mechanism to cause head movement via tail maneuvering; excellent condition; circa 1950.

Marks: Ribbon banner

Price: $595

SCHUCO YES/NO TEDDY BEAR
15 inches

Tan mohair; glass eyes; felt pads; excelsior stuffed; all jointed; near mint; 1950s.

Marks: None

Price: $1,850

CHAPTER V

SCHUCO YES/NO MUSICAL *TRICKY* TEDDY BEAR

20 inches

Beige mohair; glass eyes; excelsior stuffed; all jointed; slight wear around the key (on back) that winds the music box; circa 1950.

Marks: Tricky tag on chest

Price: Sold at Christie's, London, in 1996 for approximately $3,400.

Photo courtesy of Christie's

SCHUCO YES/NO TEDDY BEAR

5 inches

Black mohair over metal; brown glass eyes; red felt tongue; all jointed; gold foil crown; Berlin ribbon banner; mint; rare; circa 1959.

Marks: None

Price: $650-$750

BARNYARD ANIMALS

It has been my experience in over 20 years of selling soft toys that animals are almost as popular among collectors as teddy bears. In fact, a certain percentage of collectors concentrate on them totally. When studying the examples illustrated in this book it is easy to see why.

Sometimes, in our collecting fever, we tend to forget that the lovely animals we covet were originally made as children's playthings. Barnyard animals were familiar to youngsters and therefore produced in abundance. Some companies, particularly Steiff, paid great attention to detail. That attention, in itself, is a viable reason why adults find them so attractive.

STEIFF DONKEY

14 inches

Mohair; shoe button eyes; excelsior stuffed; all jointed; circa 1910.

Marks: Printed FF button

Price: $2,500

CHAPTER VI

STEIFF *LAMBY*
4 inches

White plush; glass eyes; felt ears; excelsior stuffed; mint; circa 1950s.

Marks: Chest tag

Price: $110

STEIFF *SWAPL* LAMB
8 inches

Black curly plush; open felt mouth; glass eyes; original ribbon; mint; 1950s.

Marks: Raised script button; chest tag.

Price: $395

STEIFF *JOLANTHE* PIG
12 inches

Pink mohair; felt tail and open mouth; glass eyes; excelsior stuffed; excellent condition; circa 1955.

Marks: Raised script button

Price: $290

STEIFF NAVY GOAT

9 inches

Long and short mohair; padded; ruled and wired felt horns; glass eyes; excelsior stuffed; squeaker; felt blanket with Navy mascot "N;" mint; circa 1955.

Marks: Raised script button

Price: $575

ENGLISH MERRYTHOUGHT *EEYORE*

13 inches

Mohair; plush and felt; plastic eyes; kapok stuffed; missing tail otherwise mint condition; 1960s.

Marks: Tag on foot

Price: $275

EEYORE
14 inches

Handmade from a pattern; corduroy with pasted-on features; button-on tail; soft filled; nicely made; mint; 1960s.

Marks: Makers label sewn on bottom

Price: $65-$70

STEIFF *FERDY* HORSE
6 inches

Brown and white mohair; white mane; plastic eyes; excelsior stuffed; vinyl bridle; mint; circa 1960.

Marks: Raised script button; bear head chest tag

Price: $145

STEIFF *ROCKY* GOAT
9 inches

Tan mohair; ruled, felt-covered wire horns; plastic eyes; excelsior stuffed; mint; circa 1965.

Marks: Incised button; chest tag

Price: $130-$135

BARNYARD ANIMALS

SNORT **BULL**

Red and white plush; birthday May 15, 1995

Marks: Ty hang tag; label

FLEECE **LAMB**

White plush; birthday March 21, 1996

Marks: Ty hang tag; label

QUACKERS **DUCK**

Yellow and orange plush; birthday April 19, 1994

Marks: Ty hang tag; label

INCH **THE WORM**

Varied colored plush; born September 3, 1995

Marks: Ty hang tag; label

BIRDS AND FOWL • CHAPTER VII

lthough birds and fowl were made in the 1800s, most of the examples that soft toy collectors will locate are post 1950. Colorful and charming winged friends are a welcome addition to any collection.

STEIFF DUCK
9 inches
Yellow mohair; glass eyes backed by felt; felt beak and feet; excelsior stuffed; good condition; 1920s.

Marks: None

Price: $295

BIRDS AND FOWL

STEIFF DUCK

7 inches

Airbrushed silk plush; glass eyes; felt beak and tail; excelsior stuffed; original ribbon; near mint; late 1930s-early 40s.

Marks: FF button

Price: $295

STEIFF *ADEBAR* STORK

6-1/2 inches

Felt; plastic beak; metal legs; glass eyes; excelsior stuffed; near mint; circa 1950.

Marks: Raised script button; chest tag

Price: $250

STEIFF *TULLA* GOOSE
10 inches

Mohair; felt beak and feet; glass eyes; excelsior stuffed; mint; circa 1950.

Marks; Raised script button; chest tag

Price: $400

STEIFF HEN
11 inches

Off-white mohair with realistic airbrushing; felt comb, wattle, tail, and legs; plastic eyes; excelsior stuffed; near mint; circa 1955.

Marks: Chest tag

Price: $110-$120

STEIFF *HUCKY* CROW
5 inches

Black mohair; glass eyes backed with red felt; red felt beak; metal feet; excelsior stuffed; swivel head; mint; circa 1955.

Marks: Raised script button; chest tag

Price: $90-$95

BIRDS AND FOWL

STEIFF WOOL CHICKEN
4-1/2 inches

Wooly plush; plastic eyes, beak and feet; tissue mint; late 1950s.

Marks: Bear head chest tag

Price: $60-$65

STEIFF *HUCKY* CROW
4-1/2 inches

Black mohair; felt beak, wings and eye backing; plastic eyes; tissue mint; 1950s.

Marks: Raised script button; bear head chest tag

Price: $55-$60
Shown with Steiff box.

SCHUCO PECK PECK BIRD
4 inches

Green, gray, and black mohair over metal; metal eyes, beak, feet; pecks at ground and walks when key wound; mint; circa 1950.

Marks: None

Price: $225

CHAPTER VII

STEIFF *PICCY* PELICAN
6 inches
Mohair, ruled felt feet; glass eyes; felt beak with plastic teeth; mint; 1959-1961.

Marks: Chest tag
Price: $300

STEIFF ROOSTER
10 inches
Mohair; felt tail, comb and wattle; glass eyes; excelsior stuffed; mint; 1960s.

Marks: Incised button
Price: $110

SCHUCO FINCH
3 inches
Mohair over metal; metal feet; circa 1960.

Marks: None
Price: $125

STEIFF *FRANZI* PARAKEET

5 inches

White and turquoise shaded velvet; black eyes; felt tail; plastic feet and beak; near mint; circa 1960.

Marks: Raised script button; chest tag

Price: $85-$90

STEIFF *WITTLE* OWL

9 inches

Vibrant colored mohair; felt wing tips and feet; large eyes; horschair "ears;" vinyl beak; excelsior stuffed; tissue mint; circa 1965.

Marks: Incised button; chest tag

Price: $160-$165

STEIFF PARROT AND FISH MOBILES

3 inches each

Wool; plastic feet or tails strung together on wooden bars; in cello box; circa 1970.

Marks: Incised button

Price: $250 each

STEIFF SWAN

10 inches

White plush; velour beak; felt wings; plastic eyes; softly stuffed; mint; 1980s.

Marks: Brass button; split chest tag

Price: $155-$165

STRETCH OSTRICH

Tan, brown, and white plush; birthday September 21, 1997

Marks: Ty hang tag; label

PINKY FLAMINGO

Two shades of pink plush; birthday February 13, 1995

Marks: Ty hang tag; label

PUFFER PUFFIN

Black, white, gold, and red plush; birthday November 3, 1997

Marks: Ty hang tag; label

CATS

Domestic felines have overtaken dogs as the most popular household pet. Therefore it is easy to see why collecting toy cats from various companies is a full-blown hobby. Jointed, standing, sitting or lying (and in a variety of known or imagined breeds) the collector is sure to find a host of lovable examples.

STEIFF CAT
6 inches

Felt; shoe button eyes; excelsior stuffed; remains of yarn ball between front paws; somewhat discolored; circa 1910.

Marks: None

Price: $700

GERMAN CAT

9 inches

White mohair; felt pads; glass eyes; velvet inner ears; excelsior stuffed; swivel head; pin jointed limbs; circa 1920.

Marks: None

Price: $595

OOLOO CAT

10 inches

Velvet; glass eyes; swivel head; felt tongue; mohair on tail; this cat is from the Studdy cartoon and is Bonzo's girlfriend; Chad Valley Co. Ltd England; circa 1920.

Marks: Label on foot; metal button on back

Price: $850-$900

STEIFF SIAMESE CAT

8 inches

Tan and brown mohair; blue glass eyes excelsior stuffed; swivel head; shows some wear; circa 1925.

Marks: Printed FF button

Price: $495

HELVETIC CAT

10 inches

Black and white mohair; velvet inner ears; glass eyes; swivel head; excelsior stuffed; beautiful bellows music box; circa 1930.

Marks: None

Price: $995

MERRYTHOUGHT CAT

13 inches
Creamy mohair; swivel head; painted nose; unusual set-in glass eyes that follow you; near mint; circa 1935.

Marks: Label on foot

Price: $495

APLHA FARNELL CAT

4-1/2 inches
Black mohair; horsehair tail; glass eyes; excelsior stuffed; good condition; circa 1940.

Marks: Tag on stomach

Price: $65-$75

KERSA CAT

16 inches
Gray mohair; green glass eyes; red felt boots; excelsior stuffed; all jointed; circa 1948.

Marks: Metal tag on cardboard sole.

Price: $525-$550

SCHUCO YES/NO CAT

9 inches

Off-white mohair; green and yellow mottled glass eyes; excelsior stuffed; shows wear; circa 1949.

Marks: None

Price: $495

KERSA PUSS IN BOOTS

8 inches

Black mohair; glass eyes; excelsior stuffed; felt boots; all jointed; original ribbon; some damage to boots; circa 1950.

Marks: Kersa tag on shoe sole

Price: $195

CHAPTER VIII

STEIFF KITTY
9 inches

Black and gray striped mohair; fully striped back; glass eyes; excelsior stuffed; all jointed; mint; circa 1950.

Marks: Printed FF button

Price: $495

STEIFF CAT
12 inches

Lying position; brown and white striped mohair; glass eyes; excelsior stuffed; near mint; circa 1950.

Marks: Raised script button

Price: $110

STEIFF HALLOWEEN CAT
3 inches

Black velvet with mohair tail; green glass eyes; excelsior stuffed original bow; hardest to find and most desirable of the arched position cats; near mint; circa 1950s.

Marks: Raised button; chest tag

Price: $155-$165

SCHUCO YES/NO CAT

5 inches
Gray mohair over metal armature; felt lined black mohair ears; green glass eyes; mint; circa 1955.

Marks: None

Price: $595

SCHUCO NOAH'S ARK CAT

3 inches
Mohair; pipe cleaner tail; glass eyes; metal armature; mint; circa 1955.

Marks: None

Price: $195

STEIFF *SNURRY* CAT

5 inches
White and brown striped mohair; embroidered sleep eyes; swivel head; excelsior stuffed; near mint; circa 1955.

Marks: Raised script button

Price: $195-$225

STEIFF SIAMESE CAT

4 inches
Shaded mohair; bright blue glass eyes; open velvet mouth; felt ears; excelsior stuffed; original ribbon; very hard to find; circa 1955.

Marks: None

Price: $400-$425

SCHUCO NOAH'S ARK CAT

3 inches
Shaded mohair over metal; glass eyes; all jointed; hard to find; mint; circa 1960.

Marks: None

Price: $150

TOM CAT

11 inches

Black, off-white and blue velvet; plastic eyes; firmly stuffed; from "Tom and Jerry" cartoon; made by Merrythought; 1960.

Marks: Tag on foot

Price: $150

ENGLISH MERRYTHOUGHT CAT

10 inches

White plush; blue plastic eyes; soft stuffed; 1980s.

Marks: Sewn-on label

Price: $65-$70

CHAPTER VIII

ARTIST CAT
11 inches

Made from antique buggy lap robe; glass eyes; leather pads; collar with bell; all jointed; a "Susie's Sewn Original" Creation; 1991.

Marks: Hang tag

Price: $75

POUNCE CAT

Brown and white plush; Birthday August 28, 1997

Marks: Ty hang tag; label

PRANCE CAT

Gray, black and, and white tiger stripes; birthday November 20, 1997

Marks: Ty hang tag; label

ZIP CAT

Black and white plush; birthday March 28, 1994

Marks: Ty hang tag; label

SNIP CAT

Cream and tan Siamese; birthday October 22, 1996

Marks: Ty hang tag; label

DOGS

Dog collectors are lucky - Bow Wows are easy to find. Just about every known breed can eventually be located and dogs that starred in cartoons and movies seem to have been favorite subjects of manufacturers.

STEIFF FOX TERRIER
4 inches

Velvet; shoe button eyes; excelsior stuffed; original collar; excellent condition; circa 1908.

Marks: FF button

Price: $950

CHAPTER IX

STEIFF *TIGE*
13 inches

Brown coat wool; shoe button eyes; mohair chest and front feet; excelsior stuffed; all jointed; Buster Brown's Bulldog; original muzzle; coat appears to be original to dog but not issued by Steiff; mint; circa 1910.

Marks: None

Price: $1,100

VELVET RATTLE DOG
4 inches

Airbrushed velvet; glass eyes; excelsior stuffed; original ribbon cord and bells; excellent; circa 1910.

Marks: None

Price: $695

ENGLISH BULLDOG
10 inches

Tan and black velvet; black and white glass googly eyes; jointed legs; airbrushed feet; head swivels and is also jointed at the muzzle so the head can be positioned in several ways; leather collar and horsehair ruff; probably made by Chad Valley; circa 1920.

Marks: None

Price: $1,100

Head swivels and is also jointed at the muzzle so the head can be positioned in several ways

CHAPTER IX

DISMAL DESMOND

11 inches

Flannel-like fabric; created by Dean's Rag Book of England after an illustration by George Hildebrandt; the cartoon dalmation was a woe-begone character in the 1920s; mint.

Marks: Printed data around neck including trademark of dogs pulling fabric

Price: $525

GERMAN DOG

14 inches

Tan mohair; glass eyes; excelsior stuffed; maker unknown; circa 1920.

Marks: None

Price: $425-$450

BING DOG

8 inches

Tan alpaca; glass eyes; swivel head; excelsior stuffed; mint; circa 1925.

Marks: None

Price: $375-$400

STEIFF *MOLLY* DOG

6 inches

White and cinnamon mohair; glass eyes; excelsior stuffed; swivel head; very sweet and popular dog that was in production for more than 20 years; excellent condition; circa 1929.

Marks: Printed FF button; orange stock tag

Price: $375-$400

STEIFF *BULLY* DOG

4 inches

White mohair body; black mohair head and ears with velvet inset forehead and snout; large glass eyes; studded collar (more often has a mohair ruff) with two Steiff buttons; very desirable and hard to find; circa 1928.

Marks: Printed FF button; trace of white stock tag (a total of three buttons)

Price: $475-$500

CHAPTER IX

CHAD VALLEY *BONZO*

5-1/2 inches

Velvet painted features; excellent condition; 1930s.

Marks: Button on collar

Price: $1,000

STEIFF *TREFF* DOG

4 inches

Short tan mohair; glass eyes; swivel head; excelsior stuffed; excellent condition; circa 1930.

Marks: Printed FF button

Price: $175 up

STEIFF COCKER SPANIEL

9 inches

Cinnamon and white mohair; glass eyes; swivel head; excelsior stuffed; circa 1930.

Marks: None

Price: $525

STEIFF SCOTTY DOG
10 inches

Pink mohair (color has faded from gray); glass eyes; excelsior stuffed; swivel head; side pushed squeaker; white and black leather collar; excellent condition; circa 1930.

Marks: None

Price: $650-$700

SCHUCO DOG
13 inches

Long shaggy mohair; felt lined ears; glass eyes; swivel head; excelsior stuffed; wired felt lined ears; excellent condition; circa 1935.

Marks: None

Price: $265-$275

GERMAN SPITZ DOG
12 inches

Off-white mohair; glass eyes; excelsior stuffed; near mint; circa 1935.

Marks: None

Price: $175

CHAPTER IX

STEIFF *TOSI* POODLE

10 inches

White wooly plush; swivel head; glass eyes and nose; excelsior stuffed; some wear; circa 1948.

Marks: US Zone Tag

Price: $400

STEIFF *FOXIE* DOG

6 inches

Natural shaded mohair; glass eyes; excelsior stuffed; excellent condition; hard to find in sitting position; circa 1950.

Marks: Raised script button

Price: $250 up

STEIFF *SNOBBY* POODLES

6 inches

Gray and black mohair; glass eyes and noses; felt tongues; excelsior stuffed; all jointed; collars; mint; 1950s.

Marks: Chest tag

Price: $75-$85 each

STEIFF *TESSIE* SCHNAUZER

12 inches

Gray alpaca, open velvet mouth; glass eyes; felt lined ears; swivel head; excelsior stuffed; collar; mint; circa 1950.

Marks: Chest tag

Price: $375

CHAPTER IX

STEIFF *HEXIE* DACHSOUND

5 inches

Mohair; glass googly eyes; excelsior stuffed; collar; mint; circa 1955.

Marks: Raised script button; chest tag

Price: $145

STEIFF *BAZI* DACHSOUND

8 inches

Airbrushed mohair; glass eyes; swivel head; excelsior stuffed; collar; mint; circa 1955.

Marks: Raised button; chest tag

Price: $195

STEIFF *ARCO* GERMAN SHEPARD

14 inches

Mohair; glass eyes; open felt mouth with tongue; excelsior stuffed; collar; mint; circa 1955.

Marks: Raised script button; chest tag

Price: $800

STEIFF ARCO GERMAN SHEPARD

22 inches

Airbrushed mohair; open felt mouth with tongue; glass eyes; excelsior stuffed; collar; mint; circa 1955.

Marks: Raised script button

Price: $575

SCHUCO NOAH'S ARK SCOTTY

3 inches

Black mohair over metal; felt inner ears and tongue; glass eyes; all jointed; mint; circa 1955.

Marks: None

Price: $135-$145

CHAPTER IX

PAJAMA BAG
20 inches
Grizzled gray mohair; glass eyes; zippered back; English; circa 1955.

Marks: Merrythought tag
Price: $80-$90

STEIFF *WALTHER* POODLE
11 inches
Mohair; rubber face with painted eyes; excelsior stuffed; blue leather collar; made for *Walther* Shoes; very hard to find; near mint; circa 1958.

Marks: Raised button
Price: $1,025

STEIFF *COLLIE*
16 inches
Long and short airbrushed mohair; glass eyes; open felt mouth and tongue; excelsior stuffed; near mint; circa 1960.

Marks: Chest tag
Price: $450-$475

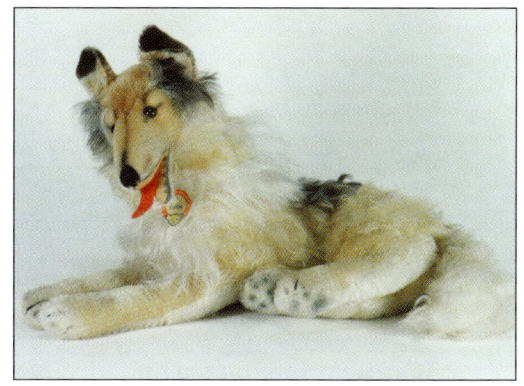

SCHUCO *LADY*

7 inches

Mohair; plastic eyes; excelsior stuffed; from the Disney movie "Lady and the Tramp" 1960s; ©Disney Enterprises.

Marks: None

Price: $225-$250

SCHUCO *TRAMP*

13 inches

Dog from "Lady and the Tramp" a Disney animated film; mohair; plastic eyes and nose; felt open mouth; leather collar; ©Disney Enterprises; 1960s.

Marks: Tag in seam

Price: $225-$250

DOG

12 inches

Plush; felt eye-backs and nose; plastic eyes; soft; circa 1965.

Marks: Hollywood Hound, Kinckerbocker Toy Co.

Price: Sentimental childhood value

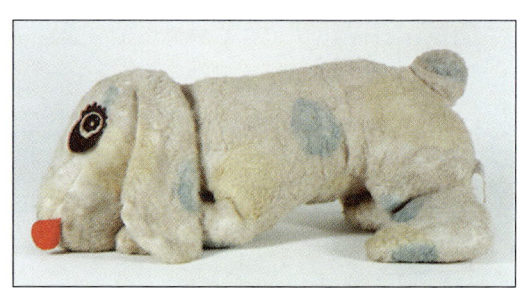

CHAPTER IX

STEIFF *BIGGIE* BEAGLE
8 inches
Realistic shaded mohair; glass eye; swivel head; excelsior stuffed; original collar; mint; circa 1965.

Marks: Incised button; chest tag
Price: $185-$190

GERMAN SHEPARD
40+ inches
Plush animal for children to lounge on; Tony Toys, England; 1990s.

Marks: Tag seam
Price: $395

BRUNO DOG
Brown and white plush terrier; birthday September 9, 1997

Marks: Ty hang tag; label

PUGSLEY DOG
Tan and brown plush pug dog; birthday May 2, 1996

Marks: Ty hang tag; label

DRESSED BEARS

Teddy bears wearing clothes, or with the clothes forming the body parts, were introduced by the major companies pre-1910. The teddies in this chapter were all issued in this manner, but it is common for collectors to outfit their own bears in charming and whimsical ways.

GERMAN WILHELM STRUNZ TEDDY BEAR

15 inches

Beige mohair head, paws and feet; shoe button eyes; black embroidered nose and claws; red embroidered mouth; excelsior stuffed; made-on navy suit (presumably a policeman's garb); note that the pin jointing is visible on all limbs; near mint; circa 1907.

Marks: None

Price: $3,000-$3,500

CHAPTER X

AMERICAN TEDDY ROOSEVELT BEAR

20 inches

Mohair head, paws, and feet; felt pads; glass eyes; all jointed; tan cotton twill fabric under the clothes; dressed in cotton twill rough rider suit; brass buttons; yellow stripe down side of trousers; leather belt; rare; circa 1907.

Marks: None

Price: $2,500

DRESSED BEARS

GERMAN UNJOINTED TEDDY BEAR

14 inches

Mohair head; glass eyes; made-on clothing; appears to be Rupert minus his scarf; circa 1930.

Marks: None

Price: $125 up

AMERICAN BANDSMAN TEDDY BEAR

20 inches (plus hat)

Plush head; glass eyes; made-on flannel clothes; removable hat; unjointed; somewhat faded; circa 1940.

Marks: None

Price: $250-$350

CHAPTER X

AMERICAN BAND MEMBER TEDDY BEAR

24 inches (including hat)

Plush head; glass eyes; felt non-removable uniform; tall felt hat; firmly stuffed; plastic trim; belt replaced; circa 1940.

Marks: None

Price: $250

AMERICAN MILITARY TEDDY BEAR

27 inches

Plush head; plastic roll around eyes; felt made-on clothes; excelsior stuffed; missing hat; circa 1940.

Marks: None

Price: $195

ENGLISH MERRYTHOUGHT *BINGIE* GUARDSMAN

11 inches

Plush; non-jointed; glass eyes; kapok stuffed; made-on clothes; removable hat; circa 1940.

Marks: Label on foot

Price: $695

GERMAN SCHUCO SOCCER TEDDY BEAR

3-1/2 inches

Mohair head; bead eyes; bendable pipe cleaner legs; felt clothes; vinyl sneakers; excellent condition; circa 1960.

Marks: None

Price: $125 up

CHAPTER X

ENGLISH MERRYTHOUGHT CHEEKY *MR. TWISTY*

9-1/2 inches

Plush head with cotton and flannel body and clothes; plastic eyes; soft stuffed; wire armature so he can "twist"; velvet inset snout; a popular version of the conventional *Cheeky*; very hard to find; near mint; 1960s.

Marks: Tagged Merrythought on foot

Price: $995

ENGLISH MERRYTHOUGHT CHEEKY *MRS. TWISTY*

10 inches

Gold mohair head; velvet muzzle; plastic eyes; felt and cotton body and clothes; soft stuffed; near mint; rare; circa 1965.

Marks: Label on foot

Price: $1,195

ENGLISH *RUPERT* TEDDY BEAR

22 inches

Plush head; vinyl humanized hands and nose; plastic eyes; soft stuffed; unjointed; made-on clothes; pull ring at side that enabled him to speak several sentences with, of course, an English accent (unfortunately this example is not working); made by Burbank Toys; circa 1965.

Marks: Tag on left side

Price: $95 (more if operating)

ENGLISH MERRYTHOUGHT GUARDSMAN TEDDY BEAR

20 inches (including hat)

Mohair head, feet and paws; made-on clothes; sewn-on hat with chain; plastic eyes; 1972.

Marks: Label on foot; hang tag

Price: $225-$245

AMERICAN SANTA *PADDINGTON* TEDDY BEAR

12 inches

Gold mohair; plastic eyes; non-jointed; dressed like Santa Claus; made by Eden; 1982.

Marks: Hang tag; data on boots

Price: $85-$100

AMERICAN APPLE TEDDY BEAR

14 inches

Polyester; unjointed; dressed in dress and shoes; Alcon Inc., boxed; 1980s.

Marks: Hang tag

Price: $55

CHAPTER X

GERMAN GEBR. HERMANN TEDDIES
12 inches

Non-jointed plush; dressed as an Alpine girl and boy; 1983.

Marks: Hang tag

Price: $80 up each

AMERICAN GUND *BIALOSKY* TEDDY BEAR
24 inches

Plush; velour pads; firmly; stuffed; plastic eyes; all jointed; sweater with logo and beany; signed on tag by Peggy and Alan Bialosky; mint; 1983.

Marks: Paper ear tag

Price: $495

AMERICAN GUND *BIALOSKY* TEDDY BEAR
18 inches

Plush; plastic eyes; felt pads; all jointed; wearing a flight jacket and scarf; mint; 1980s.

Marks: Sewn-in label

Price: $375

DRESSED BEARS

ENGLISH MERRYTHOUGHT *GUARDSMAN* TEDDY BEAR

17 inches

Mohair head, paws and feet; swivel head; plastic eyes; made-on clothes; removable hat; mint; 1985.

Marks: Label; hang tag

Price: $195 up

AMERICAN PATRIOT TEDDY BEAR

18 inches

Plush; dressed as a U.S. Postal carrier; made by J.J. Wind Inc.© 1986.

Marks: Seam tag; hang tag

Price: $195 up

CHAPTER X

ENGLISH *PADDINGTON* TEDDY BEAR
18 inches

Gold mohair; plastic eyes and nose; non-jointed; dressed in felt with rubber boots; made by Gabrielle Designs Ltd. In 1980s.

Marks: Hang tag and data on Wellington soles

Price: $175

ENGLISH MERRYTHOUGHT TEDDY BEAR
15 inches

Gold mohair; plastic eyes; felt and plush trim clothes; designed for Christmas; M.I.B. 1980s.

Marks: Label on foot

Price: $350

AMERICAN RUSS BERRIE *BENJAMIN*
20 inches

Curly plush; plastic eyes; unjointed; dressed in shirt and blouse; mint; 1980s.

Marks: Hang tag in ear

Price: $80

ENGLISH TEDDY BEAR
30 inches

Unjointed plush; plastic eyes; beautifully dressed in Scot's outfit; leather shoes; made by Arlesford; mint; 1980s.

Marks: Hang tag

Price: $495

ENGLISH CHARACTER TEDDY BEAR
30 inches

Dressed like a Guardsman in fine detail; plush; nonjointed; soft stuffed; plastic eyes and nose; made by Alresford; 1983.

Marks: Paper hang tag

Price: $495

ENGLISH NURSE TEDDY BEAR

30 inches

Plush; plastic eyes and nose; soft stuffed; non-jointed; beautifully costumed in cotton dress, hat and apron; lined wool cape; leather shoes; made by Alresford; 1983.

Marks: Paper hang tag

Price: $495

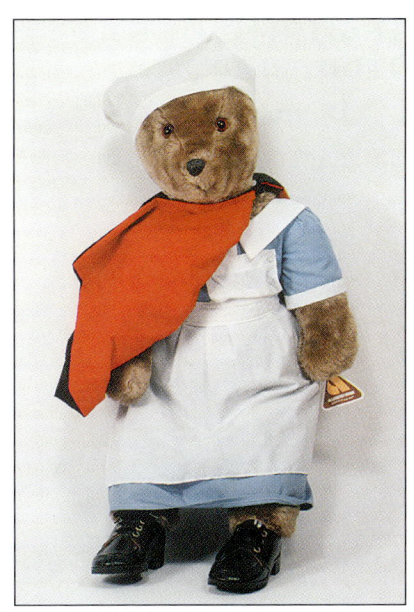

ENGLISH "BOBBY" TEDDY BEAR

30 inches

Plush; plastic eyes and nose; soft stuffed; non-jointed; beautiful wool costume; leather shoes; made by Alresford; 1983.

Marks: Paper hang tag

Price: $495

ENGLISH LITTLE FOLK TEDDY BEAR

12 inches

Unjointed plush; plastic eyes; vinyl nose; cotton dress; mint; 1980s.

Marks: Tag on arm

Price: $85

S.S. NISBET ENGLISH TEDDY BEAR

14 inches

Brown alpaca; plastic eyes; all jointed; sailor middy and hat; made by Nisbets of England; mint; 1980s.

Marks: Paper hang tags

Price: $175

ENGLISH MERRYTHOUGHT *BEEFEATER* TEDDY BEAR

17 inches

Mohair head, paws and feet; swivel head; plastic eyes; made-on clothes; removable hat; mint; 1985.

Marks: Label; hang tag

Price: $195

CHAPTER X

ENGLISH MERRYTHOUGHT *HIGHLANDER* TEDDY BEAR

17 inches

Mohair head and paws; swivel head; plastic eyes; made-on clothes; removable hat; mint; 1986.

Marks: Label; hang tag

Price: $225-$250

SHAKESBEAR AND CYRANO DE BEARJERAC

20 inches

Velour with stain and velvet clothing; two of several "play on words" bears by the North American Bear Co.; 1980s.

Marks: Seam tags

Price: $295 each

MUFFY VANDERBEAR

7 inches

Dressed in christening gown and hat; North American Bear Co.; 1980s.

Marks: Seam tag; hang tag

Price: $35

HEIDI OTT TEDDY BEAR
9-1/2 inches
Rubber head and limbs; bean bag body; dressed in a variety of costumes and in a presentation box; 1990s.

Marks: Paper hang tag

Price: $40-$50

HEIDI OTT TEDDY BEAR
9-1/2 inches
Rubber head and limbs; bean bag body; dressed attractively; a variety of clothing styles and bear colors are available; in a presentation box; 1990s.

Marks: Hang tag

Price: $40

ENGLISH *RUPERT* TEDDY BEAR
7 inches
White plush head, paws and feet; made-on clothes; removable scarf; soft stuffed; produced by Ashley House; 1992.

Marks: Tag on left side

Price: $10-$15

CHAPTER X

ENGLISH MERRYTHOUGHT *QUEEN ELIZABETH I* TEDDY BEAR
10 inches

Mohair; plastic eyes; soft stuffed; all jointed; lovely period clothes; mint; 1990s.

Marks: Labels; hang tags

Price: $200

GERMAN HERMANN SPIELWAREN TEDDY BEAR
7 inches

Gold mohair; plastic eyes; soft stuffed; non-jointed; dressed in Tyrolean costumes; 1993.

Marks: Label and hang tag

Price: $75 each

Susan Stanton-Reid Collection

DRESSED DOLLS AND ANIMALS

Soft dolls, dressed in a detailed fashion, were introduced by the Steiff Company in 1902. Many other companies, including Steiff, continued to produce a variety of attired animals and bears over the years. Cartoon characters clothed in recognizable couture are a special feature.

STEIFF *NIKOLAS*

20 inches

Felt; with mohair trim on the cloak; all jointed including moveable knee sockets; glass eyes; from a character in the book *Struwwelpeter*; 1911.

Marks: FF button; trace of white tag

Price: $3,500 up

CHAPTER XI

STEIFF *HANSILI* RABBIT
8 inches

Mohair; glass eyes; cotton body; cotton and felt clothes; swivel head; excelsior stuffed; shows wear; 1920s.

Marks: FF button

Price: $795

STEIFF *MICKEY MOUSE*
13 inches

Velvet; pie shaped eyes; felt ears; non-removable clothes; slight graying to face; excellent condition; 1920s; ©Disney Enterprises.

Marks: FF button; trace of orange stock tag; chest tag

Price: $6,100

SCHUCO YES/NO DWARF

9 inches

Felt; shoe button eyes; mohair hair and hat; excelsior stuffed; all jointed; red felt circle under hat; velvet pants; excellent; circa 1925.

Marks: None

Price: $850

STEIFF *VERA*

15 inches

Celluloid head painted from the inside; felt body; all jointed; original cotton clothes; a Schlopsnies design; mint; 1921-1925 only.

Marks: Hang tag

Price: $4,000

STEIFF *LUCIE*

13 inches

Molded felt face; felt all jointed body; glass eyes; cotton and felt clothes; mint; 1930s.

Marks: Hang tag

Price: $2,200

CHAPTER XI

STEIFF *MICKEY* AND *MINNIE MOUSE*

12 inches

Velvet; felt; pie shaped eyes; Minnie has an open mouth; very hard to find size; excellent condition; ©Disney Enterprises; circa 1930.

Marks: Chest tag on Mickey; button and trace of orange tag on Minnie

Price: $7,500 pair up

SCHUCO DWARF

14 inches

Plastic face; pipe cleaner limbs; felt clothes; a *Snow White* product; mint; ©Disney Enterprises; 1940s.

Marks: None

Price: $175

DRESSED DOLLS AND ANIMALS

OSKAR CAT
8 inches

Made by Gbr. Hermann of Germany; composition head; mohair and felt body; dressed in trousers, sweater, and tie; missing pipe; hard to find; 1950s.

Marks: Tag attached to pants

Price: $250 up

STEIFF *NIKILI* RABBIT
8 inches (plus ears)

Off-white mohair; open felt mouth; glass eyes; jointed head and arms; non-removable felt shoes; felt trousers and vest; cotton print tie; mint; circa 1950.

Marks: None

Price: $295-$325

STEIFF *WALDILI* DACHSHOUND
10 inches

Mohair head, paws and feet; felt pads; glass eyes; excelsior stuffed; swivel head; felt clothes; wooden rifle; mint; 1950s.

Marks: Raised script button; chest tag

Price: $425-$475

CHAPTER XI

STEIFF *PUCKI, LUCKI AND GUCKI* DWARVES

7 inches

Rubber heads; felt limbs and clothes; all jointed; mohair wigs and beards; vinyl shoes; mint; 1950s.

Marks: Raised script buttons and chest tags

Price: $150 each

STEIFF *MICKI, MECKI AND MACKI*

7 inches and 4-1/2 inches

Rubber faces; Micki and Mecki have felt bodies; Macki all rubber; mohair wigs; cotton and felt clothes; mint; 1950s.

Marks: Chest tags, raised script buttons

Price: $90 (Micki and Mecki); $75 (Macki)

DRESSED DOLLS AND ANIMALS

SCHUCO MOUSE
10 inches

Mohair; plastic eyes; felt nose, mouth and clothes; from the Disney movie "Cinderella;" ©Disney Enterprices; circa 1960.

Marks: None

Price: $395

STEIFF *SANDY* DOLL
11 inches

Rubber face; felt clothes; mohair wig; mint; circa 1960.

Marks: Raised script button on wrist bracelet; chest tag

Price: $225

STEIFF *CAPPY* DOLL
11 inches

Rubber face; felt hands, shoes and hat; rayon suit with bells; mint; circa 1960.

Marks: Raised script button on wrist bracelet; chest tag

Price: $195

CHAPTER XI

SCHUCO *GOOFY*

14 inches

Mohair head and feet; glass eyes; felt ears, gloves and shirt; cotton pants; ©Disney Enterprises; near mint; circa 1960.

Marks: Bigo Belo tag sewn on

Price: $235 up

KERSA DWARVES

8 inches

Molded felt faces; felt construction with non-removable clothes; names are Ruck, Muck, Bam, Troll, Bum, Himpel and Puck; mint; circa 1960.

Marks: Kersa metal plates on soles; paper hang tags

Price: $75 each

GERMAN *STRUWWELPETER*
18 inches (including hair)

Felt with painted features; toothpick "fingernails" and wild hair; felt stockings; ribbon tie-on sandals; felt clothes; based on a book by Dr. Heinrich Hoffman; story of a shock head boy who let his hair go wild; possibly East German; circa 1960.

Marks: None

Price: $350-$400

POOH'S FRIEND *PIGLET*
10 inches (plus ears)

Flesh colored flannel; plastic eyes; soft stuffed; removable flannel clothes; made in England by Merrythought; excellent condition; 1960s.

Marks: Tag on bottom of foot

Price: $395-$400

R. JOHN WRIGHT *ST. NIKOLAS*
17 inches

Molded felt; painted features; felt clothes; wooden staff; basket; mint; 1981.

Marks: Paper hang tag

Price: $1,700

CHAPTER XI

ALICE AND THE *JABBERWOCKY*

11 inches and 9 inches

Plastic doll and fabric animal; made by Madame Alexander for the 1993 Disney World Convention; M.I.B.

Marks: Tags

Price: $495

STEIFF *MICKEY MOUSE*

14 inches

Mohair, velvet and velour; bendable; made for La Maison de Donaldson in Belguim; Ltd edition of 2,000; 1997; M.I.B.; ©Disney Enterprises.

Marks: Brass button; white stock tag; hang tag booklet; certificate

Price: $595

FOREST AND GARDEN CREATURES

Bunnies, fox, squirrels, bats, badgers, moose, deer and lady bugs are familiar creatures to us all. Their counterparts in the soft toy world are sure to please.

FOX

12 inches

Reddish gold mohair; shoe button eyes; excelsior stuffed; swivel head; maker unknown; circa 1910.

Marks: None

Price: $600 up

CHAPTER XII

STEIFF FOX

6-1/2 inches (plus tail)

Orange, white and black (tip on ears) mohair; glass eyes; excelsior stuffed; all jointed; excellent condition; circa 1920.

Marks: None

Price: $475 up

STEIFF TAIL TURNS HEAD RABBIT

8 inches (plus ears)

Mohair; glass eyes; excelsior stuffed; head turns in a circular motion by rotating the tail; mint; 1920s.

Marks: FF button; partial red tag

Price: $2,400

Hang tag on Steiff Rabbit's tail explaining mechanical movement.

FOREST AND GARDEN CREATURES

STEIFF SQUIRREL
7 inches

Faded mohair; black glass eyes backed by felt; all jointed including the tail; good condition; circa 1920.

Marks: None

Price: $245

STEIFF SQUIRREL
7 inches

Mohair; excelsior stuffed; velvet nut; near mint; 1930s-1959s.

Marks: None

Price: $100

CHAPTER XII

STEIFF *ERIC* BAT

4 inches

Mohair body and head; pipe cleaner limbs; glass eyes and nose; felt ears; irredescent vinyl wings; tissue mint; 1950s.

Marks: Raised script button; stock tag; chest tag

Price: $395-$425

STEIFF *SPIDY*

4 inches

Colorful airbrushed mohair; pipe cleaner legs; three bead eyes; excelsior stuffed; tissue mint; 1950s.

Marks: Raised script button; stock tag; chest tag

Price: $295-$325

KERSA RABBIT

6-1/2 inches plus ears

Plush head; glass eyes; felt clothes; excelsior stuffed with some wire and cotton in limbs; charming laced shoes; mint condition; 1950s.

Marks: Kersa tag on shoe sole

Price: $120

FOREST AND GARDEN CREATURES

KERSA GIRL RABBIT
12-1/2 inches plus ears

Felt; felt and cotton clothes; glass eyes; excelsior stuffed; basket on back somewhat worn; 1950s.

Marks: Kersa tag on shoe sole

Price: $195

KERSA BOY RABBITT
10 inches plus ears

Felt; felt and cotton clothes; shirt missing; cardboard on shoe repaired.

Marks: Kersa tag on shoe sole

Price: $120

KERSA RABBIT
10 inches

Brown wool plush head; peach felt body; black glass eyes; excelsior stuffed; cotton clothes; "grass" filled basket on back; holds an artist's palette; mint; rare; circa 1950.

Marks: Metal plate on left sole

Price: $285

STEIFF *DIGGY* BADGER
5-1/2 inches

Black, white and orange mohair; felt feet; glass eyes; excelsior stuffed; mint; circa 1957.

Marks: Bear head chest tag

Price: $185-$195

SCHUCO LADY BUG
3 inches including feelers

Red, black and white mohair; pipe cleaner feelers and six legs; firmly stuffed; mint; circa 1959.

Marks: None

Price: $95

GEBR. HERMANN SQUIRREL
5 inches

Long and short mohair; glass eyes; felt lined ears; excelsior stuffed; swivel head; good condition; circa 1950.

Marks: None

Price: $25-$35

STEIFF *MANNI* RABBIT

10 inches

Airbrushed mohair; swivel head; open felt mouth; excelsior stuffed; glass eyes; original ribbon; mint; circa 1950.

Marks: Raised script button; chest tag

Price: $250

STEIFF RUNNING RABBIT

7 inches

Airbrushed mohair; glass eyes; excelsior stuffed; original ribbon; mint; circa 1955.

Marks: Raised script button; chest tag; FAO Schwarz tag

Price: $140-$145

SCHUCO FOX

10 inches

Red and white long and short mohair; glass eyes; plastic nose; felt inner ears; swivel head; excelsior stuffed; excellent condition; 1950s.

Marks: None

Price: $125 up

CHAPTER XII

STEIFF *MOOSY*
10 inches

Brown mohair; felt padded and wired antlers; glass eyes; excelsior stuffed; mint; circa 1955.

Marks: Raised script button; chest tag

Price: $595-$625

STEIFF *TIMMY* RABBIT
7 inches

Black and white dralon; glass eyes; hard and soft stuffed; mint; circa 1965.

Marks: Incised button; chest tag

Price: $140-$145

SCHUCO *THUMPER* RABBIT
9-1/2 inches

Mohair; plastic eyes, nose; felt open mouth and teeth; part of the Bigo Belo series; near mint; circa 1960.

Marks: None

Price: $400

SCHUCO RABBIT

14 inches

Mohair; open mouth with felt teeth; plastic eyes; excelsior and soft stuffed; bendable mint; circa 1960.

Marks: Bigo Belo tag

Price: $125 up

GRISLY RABBIT

15 inches plus ears

Gold long and short mohair; glass eyes; open felt mouth; soft and excelsior stuffed; wired ears; all jointed; circa 1960.

Marks: Metal button on left chest; tag in right arm

Price: $115-$120

GRISLY RABBIT

8 inches

Brown mohair; glass eyes; floss nose and mouth; excelsior stuffed; mint; circa 1960.

Marks: Grisly button on side; plastic tag in back

Price: $80-$85

SCHUCO RABBIT

13-3/4 inches

Tan shaded long and short mohair head, arms and feet; striped cotton legs; cotton pants; jersey shirt; glass eyes; soft and hard stuffed; near mint; 1960s.

Marks: Schuco Bigo Belo paper tag

Price: $185

STEIFF *HÖRNI* SQUIRREL

13 inches

Rust dralon plush; open mouth with felt teeth; plastic eyes; cotton clothing; felt hat; Promotional safety guard; late 1970s.

Marks: Brass button

Price: $125

FOREST AND GARDEN CREATURES

STEIFF *PERRI* SQUIRREL
8 inches
Tipped mohair; plastic eyes; holds acorn between mohair paws; ©Disney Enterprises; mint; circa 1972.

STEIFF *PERRI* SQUIRREL
5-1/2 inches
Same description except paws are made of felt.

STEIFF *PERRI* SQUIRREL
4 inches
Same description as middle size except does not hold acorn.

Marks: Incised button; split chest tags

Prices: $95-$175

STEIFF *ELFI* FAWN

15 inches

Tan spotted dralon plush; plastic eyes; mint; circa 1982.

Marks: Brass button; split chest tag

Price: $225-$240

STEIFF RABBIT

30 inches

Brown and white plush; plastic eyes; open felt mouth with two teeth; soft stuffed; long dangly legs (like Lulac.); mint; circa 1985.

Marks: Brass button

Price: $300-$325

FOREST AND GARDEN CREATURES

FLOPPITY RABBIT

Lavendar plush; birthday May 28, 1996

Marks: Ty hang tag; label

EARS RABBIT

Brown and white plush; birthday April 18, 1995

Marks: Ty hang tag; label

IGGY IGUANA

Tie dyed; birthday August 12, 1997

Marks: Ty hang tag; label

HISSY SNAKE

Yellow and blue plush; red tongue; birthday April 4, 1997

Marks: Ty hang tag; label

RAINBOW CHAMELEON

Tie dyed; borthday October 14, 1997

Marks: Ty hang tag; label

SLY FOX

Cinnamon and white plush; birthday September 12, 1996

Marks: Ty Hang tag; label

RINGO RACCOON

Tan, brown and white plush; birthday July 14, 1995

Marks: Ty hang tag; label

KOALAS, PANDAS AND POLAR BEARS • CHAPTER XIII

There was a time when pandas were not recognized as bears (except by collectors). Now we know that they are indeed of the ursine family and many collectors concentrate on them with great zeal.

ENGLISH DEAN'S PANDA BEAR
11 inches
Black and white mohair; glass eyes; velvet pads with four fingers on the front paws; kapok stuffed; all jointed; shows some wear; 1930s.

Marks: Fabric tag on foot

Price: $900

KOALAS, PANDAS, AND POLAR BEARS

STEIFF PANDA BEAR
12 inches

Black and white mohair; open felt mouth; felt pads; all jointed; excelsior stuffed; excellent condition; circa 1950.

Marks: Raised script button

Price: $750

ENGLISH PANDA BEAR
19 inches

Black and white mohair; glass eyes; excelsior and kapok stuffed; all jointed; near mint; made by Pedigree; circa 1950.

Marks: Partial label in seam

Price: $250 up

Susan Stanton-Reid Collection

STEIFF PANDY INDIAN PANDA
8 inches plus tail

White, black and orange mohair; plastic eyes; felt claws; swivel head; excelsior stuffed; hard to find size; mint; 1950s.

Marks: Chest tag

Price: $350-$360

STEIFF KOALAS
5 inches and 9 inches

Tan and white mohair; glass eyes; felt feet and nose on small; felt nose on larger; excelsior stuffed; all jointed; mint; 1950s.

Marks: Raised script buttons; chest tag on 5 inch

Price: Small $450 up
Large $550 up

ENGLISH PANDA BEAR
15 inches

Black and white plush; cotton foot pads; plastic eyes; soft stuffed; unjointed; near mint; made by Wendy Boston; circa 1960.

Marks: Sewn on label

Price: $100

Susan Stanton-Reid Collection

KOALAS, PANDAS, AND POLAR BEARS

ENGLISH PANDA BEAR
14 inches

Black and white plush; plastic eyes; shaped fabric nose; non-jointed; soft stuffed; white claws; realistic conformation; made by Wendy Boston; near mint; circa 1960.

Marks: Sewn on label

Price: $75 up

Susan Stanton-Reid Collection

STEIFF POLAR BEAR
11 inches

White plush; black plastic eyes; felt feet; soft stuffed; excellent condition; circa 1968.

Marks: None

Price: $55-$65

STEIFF *COSY* KOALA
4 inches

Plush; plastic eyes; felt paws; swivel head; near mint; 1970s.

Marks: Chest tag

Price: $85

CHAPTER XIII

ENGLISH POLAR BEAR
16 inches
White plush; plastic eyes; soft stuffed; made by Alresford; 1983.

Marks: Paper tag; sewn on label

Price: $80

PANDA
9 inches
Plush; battery operated; walks and eyes light up; souvenir from Beijing Zoo; 1990s.

Marks: None

Price: $25-$35

PUPPETS

Children, especially, love to play with hand puppets, but I know adult collectors who try to amass every one made. Fortunately a wonderful selection is possible to attain.

ENGLISH *FELIX* CAT PUPPET
8 inches

Black and white mohair; shoe button eyes backed by felt; felt mouth; embroidered teeth; excellent condition; circa 1920.

Marks: None

Price: $75

CHAPTER XIV

ENGLISH FARNELL MONKEY PUPPET

8 inches

Brown mohair; felt face, ears and paws; glass eyes; painted lids; near mint; circa 1930.

Marks: Cloth label

Price: $135

STEIFF LION CUB PUPPET

9 inches

Wooly fabric; glass eyes; excelsior stuffed head; mint; circa 1950.

Marks: Raised script button

Price: $100

PUPPETS

STEIFF *SMARDY* FOX HAND PUPPET
10 inches

Cinnamon, white and black mohair; airbrushed features; plastic eyes; tissue mint; shown with puppet stand of the same era; circa 1960.

Marks: Button; chest tag

Price: $110-$115 with stand

STEIFF KITTY HAND PUPPET
9 inches

White and gray striped mohair; plastic eyes; original ribbon; tissue mint; circa 1969.

Marks: Incised button; split chest tag

Price: $80-$90

STEIFF HIDE-A-GIFT CAT
5 inches

Mohair head and arms; felt dress; hollow under skirt to conceal small presents; mint; circa 1955.

Marks: Raised script button; chest tag

Price: $110-$125

CHAPTER XIV

STEIFF HAND PUPPETS

Over the years, Steiff has produced puppets as a staple product; a variety for the 1970s in shown.

Marks: Incised buttons; split chest tags

Price: $75 up depending on production figure

AMERICAN HAND PUPPET

11 inches

Black plush; plastic eyes; open interior to allow nose movement as well as realistic body scampering; fun for children of all ages; circa 1979.

Marks: Furry Folk Hand Puppets, Ca.

Price: $80-$90

PUPPETS

STEIFF *JOLLY SKUNK* ARM PUPPET

14 inches

Black, gray and white plush; plastic eyes; hollow body; mint; 1980s.

Marks: Brass button; split chest tag

Price: $155

ENGLISH *RUPERT* HAND PUPPET

10 inches

White plush head and paws; cotton shirt; yellow scarf; made by Pedigree; 1980s.

Marks: Label on back of head

Price: $30-$35

WATER FRIENDLY ANIMALS • CHAPTER XV

Beavers building their dams, penguins waddling, frogs croaking, turtles being slow and even the Loch Ness Monster evoke water memories. Companies recognized this need and made it possible to achieve soft toy examples in many forms.

ENGLISH LOCH NESS MONSTER
11 inches
Green and gold velvet; clear glass eyes; kapok stuffed; wears plaid neck bow and tam o' shanter; made by Dean's Rag Book; near mint; circa 1930.

Marks: Button on underside

Price: $325

STEIFF *NAGY* BEAVERS

4 inches, 10 inches and 6 inches

Mohair; felt paws and feet; felt teeth; airbrushed toes; glass eyes; swivel heads; excelsior stuffed; mint; 1950s.

Marks: Raised script cript buttons; chest tags

Price: $110, $195, $155

SCHUCO YES/NO PENGUIN

7-1/2 inches
Mohair; felt beak and feet; levering tail produces a yes/no movement; 1950s.

Marks: None

Price: $750

CHAPTER XV

STEIFF *ROBBY* SEAL

8 inches

Mohair; glass eyes; excelsior stuffed; mint; 1950s.

Marks: Chest tag

Price: $110-$125

STEIFF *FROGGY*

5 inches

Green and pale gold velvet; airbrushed markings; plastic eyes; excelsior stuffed; mint condition; 1960s.

Marks: Incised button; chest tag

Price: $90-$100

SCHUCO NOAH'S ARK TURTLE

3 inches

Mohair body; pipe cleaner head, feet and tail; mint; circa 1960.

Marks: None

Price: $125

STEIFF *SLO* TURTLE
13 inches

Colorful airbrushed mohair; open felt mouth; plastic eyes; hard and soft stuffed; tissue mint; circa 1969.

Marks: Incised button; chest tag

Price: $225

SMOOCHY FROG

Green and gold plush; birthday October 1, 1996

Marks: Ty hang tag; label

SEAWEED OTTER

Tan and brown plush; birthday March 19, 1996

Marks: Ty hang tag; label

WHEELED BEARS AND ANIMALS • CHAPTER XVI

Animals and bears on wheels happen to be among my personal favorites. To me, they present an old world feeling. Of course the larger ones love to give teddy bears a ride.

STEIFF DUCK ON WHEELS
11 inches long

Gray velvet with black and pale teal airbrushing; gold beak; orange felt feet in swimming position; shoe button eyes; cotton stuffed; near mint; pictured in 1908 catalog.

Marks: None

Price: $950 up

WHEELED BEARS AND ANIMALS

ELEPHANT ON WHEELS
13 inches

Gray felt; red felt blanket; shoe button eyes; cast wheels painted bronze; resembles Steiff in some ways; possibly English; circa 1910.

Marks: None

Price: $765-$785

STEIFF CAMEL ON CAST WHEELS
10 inches

Mohair; shoe button eyes; excelsior stuffed; original harness and blanket; circa 1910.

Marks: None

Price: $950

STEIFF ST. BERNARD ON WHEELS
16 inches long

Long curly white and brown mohair; brown glass eyes; excelsior stuffed; pull bark still operating; on cast iron wheels; near mint; circa 1910.

Marks: Printed FF button

Price: $950 up

STEIFF COW ON WHEELS

11 inches

White felt with airbrushed markings; shoe button eyes; excelsior stuffed; leather collar; metal wheels; near mint; circa 1910.

Marks: Printed FF button with full white stock tag

Price: $1,600

STEIFF MONKEY ON ECCENTRIC WHEELS

8 inches

Rust and tan felt; shoe button eyes; excelsior stuffed; bell at neck ruff; replaced tail; some soiling; varnished wheels that are offset to produce hopping action; circa 1912.

Marks: Printed FF button

Price: $400 up depending on condition

STEIFF DACHSHOUND ON ECCENTRIC WHEELS

15 inches

Brown felt with airbrushing; glass eyes; excelsior stuffed; wheels off-set to produce hopping action; mint; circa 1915.

Marks: Printed FF button; trace of white stock tag

Price: $1,100-$1,200

BING TRIP TRAP ELEPHANT

9 inches

Off-white mohair head and tail; felt fabric (over metal legs) form the yellow dotted clown costume; hat with pom pom; silk cord trim; shoe button eyes backed by felt; walks by means of small wheels in feet; circa 1920.

Marks: None

Price: $995

STEIFF RECORD PETER

9 inches

Felt with made-on clothes; mohair head; black glass eyes; airbrushed nose and mouth; when pulled the cart goes up and down; metal cart with wooden wheels; original pull string; near mint; circa 1920.

Marks: Printed FF button

Price: $1,400 up

STEIFF HORSE AND CART ON WHEELS

21 inches (horse)

Fabric horse; glass eyes; excelsior stuffed; horsehair mane and tail; felt blanket; beautiful leather saddle and trappings; wooden wagon; excellent condition; circa 1920.

Marks: None

Price: $1,800

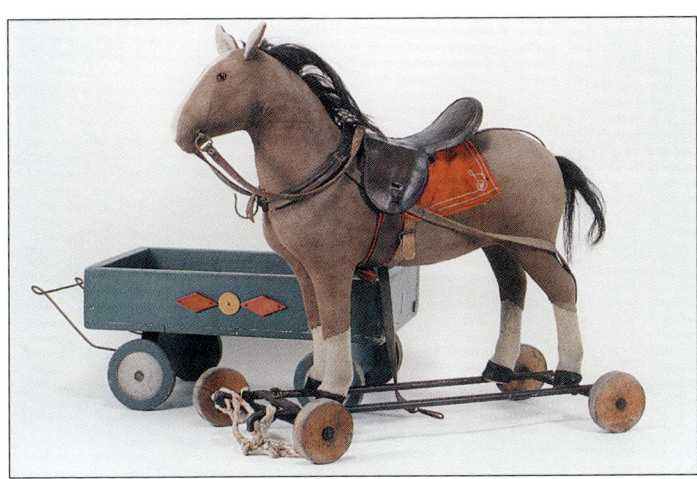

SCHUCO BEAR ON WHEELS
10 inches

Tipped brown mohair; glass eyes; swivel head; excelsior stuffed; felt pads; metal frame and wheels; near mint; circa 1925.

Marks: None

Price: $895

ENGLISH LAMB ON WHEELS
21 inches

Sheepskin over metal frame; blue glass eyes set into lids; leather hooves; rubber tired wheels; mint; circa 1935.

Marks: None

Price: $975

RECORD HANSI
9 inches

Tan mohair; glass eyes; excelsior stuffed; cart goes up and down as rabbit is pulled; near mint; 1950s.

Marks: Raised script button

Price: $1,000

WILD ANIMALS • CHAPTER XVII

I f it's not possible to go on safari, the wild beasts in the soft toy world can be your own personal Africa.

STEIFF ELEPHANT

12 inches

Off-white mohair; shoe button eyes; excelsior stuffed; felt tusks; all jointed; mint; circa 1910.

Marks: FF button; white stock tag

Price: $2,700

MERRYTHOUGHT *GRAN'POP* MONKEY
26 inches

Gold mohair; molded and painted velvet; brown velvet inner ears, paws, and feet; excelsior stuffed; all jointed; near mint; designed by artist Lawson Wood; circa 1930.

Marks: Label on foot

Price: $895

CHAD VALLEY ELEPHANT
10 inches

Off-white mohair; glass eyes; felt tusks; excelsior stuffed; near mint; circa 1930.

Marks: Sewn-on label

Price: $155

MERRYTHOUGHT *GRAN'POP* MONKEY
13 inches

Gold mohair; velvet face and feet; printed featured; kapok stuffed; all jointed; a Lawson Wood design; mint; 1930.

Marks: Tag on foot

Price: $400

MERRYTHOUGHT MONKEY
13 inches

Alpaca; painted velvet face; velvet hands, feet and inner ears; kapok stuffed; all jointed; designed by Lawson Woods for Merrythought; mint; circa 1938.

Marks: Tag on foot

Price: $295-$325

STEIFF TIGER
20 inches

Realistic striped mohair; glass eyes; excelsior stuffed; very good condition; circa 1947.

Marks: Printed trailing FF button

Price: $185-$195

SCHUCO YES/NO MONKEY
11 inches

Mohair; felt face, ears and paws; shows wear on face; all jointed; circa 1948.

Marks: Tricky tag

Price: $200-$225

SCHUCO YES/NO ORANGUTAN
17 inches

Long, curly rust mohair; felt face, ears, feet, and hands; glass eyes set in lids; excellent condition; circa 1948.

Marks: None

Price: $550

GERMAN ELEPHANT
5 inches

Pink plush; glass googly eyes; excelsior stuffed; near mint; possible Schuco; circa 1948.

Marks: U S Zone tag

Price: $90-$95

SCHUCO YES/NO ELEPHANT
5 inches

Mohair over metal; glass eyes; felt ears and tusks; all jointed; mint; 1950s.

Marks: None

Price: $525

CHAPTER XVI

STEIFF *COCO* BABBOON

14 inches (sitting)

Gray curly mohair; felt face, ears and paws; open mouth with airbrushing; horsehair mantle; glass eyes; excelsior stuffed; all jointed; mint; circa 1950.

Marks: Raised script button

Price: $495

STEIFF LLAMA

10 inches

Long and short airbrushed mohair; glass eyes; excelsior stuffed; mint; circa 1950.

Marks: Raised script button

Price: $275

STEIFF *RENNY* REINDEER

6 inches

Airbrushed tan mohair; glass eyes; double weight felt antlers; excelsior stuffed; circa 1950.

Marks: Bear head chest tag

Price: $115-$125

TIGER

10-1/2 inches

Bristle plush; painted stripes; glass eyes; excelsior stuffed; Japanese; circa 1950.

Marks: None

Price: $10-$15

TIGGER

13 inches

Agnes Brush design; painted fabric; string whiskers; cotton stuffed; excellent condition; 1950s.

Marks: None

Price: $475

CHAPTER XVII

STEIFF RECLINING TIGER
29 inches
Realistic striped mohair; green glass eyes; excelsior stuffed; mint; rare size; 1950s.

Marks: Raised script button
Price: $650

STEIFF DANGLING TIGER
32 inches
Realistic striped mohair; green glass eyes; excelsior stuffed; long legs; a novelty made for a short time; mint; 1950s.

Marks: Raised script button
Price: $1,700

Courtesy Michelle Dauton

STEIFF CAMEL
13 inches
Wooly plus and velvet; glass eyes; excelsior stuffed; mint; circa 1955.

Marks: Raised script button
Price: $345

SCHUCO NOAH'S ARK ELEPHANT

3 inches

Gray mohair; bead eyes; felt ears and tusks; all jointed; metal armature; original blanket; mint; circa 1955.

Marks: None

Price: $195

STEIFF *LEA* LIONESS

4 inches

Mohair; glass eyes; excelsior stuffed; mint; circa 1955.

Marks: Chest tag

Price: $175

SCHUCO NOAH'S ARK LION

3 inches

Gold mohair over metal; glass eyes; all jointed; mint; circa 1955.

Marks: None

Price: $135-$145

STEIFF *RENNY* REINDEER

9 inches

Off-white and brown airbrushed mohair; glass eyes; padded and wired antlers; squeaker; excelsior stuffed; stitch on nose to highlight; mint; circa 1955.

Marks: Chest tag

Price: $285-$295

STEIFF COSY CAMEL

5-1/2 inches

Tan wooly plush; velvet face and legs; felt ears; glass eyes; excelsior stuffed; near mint; circa 1958.

Marks: Chest tag

Price: $85-$90

MERRYTHOUGHT *TIGGER*

10 inches

Short napped plush; airbrushed stripes; glass eyes; kapok stuffed; excellent condition; 1960s.

Marks: Sewn-on label

Price: $275

FELT TIGER

11 inches

Orange felt with glued on black felt stripes and eyes; soft stuffed; internal chime-sounding rattle; origin unknown; circa 1960.

Marks: None

Price: $35-$40

MERRYTHOUGHT *KANGA AND ROO*

13 inches and 4-1/2 inches

Mohair animals from the Winnie-the-Pooh series; made by Merrythought in England in the 1960s; near mint.

Marks: Label on foot

Price: $225

SCHUCO MONKEY

14 inches

Bigo Belo Orangutan; felt and mohair; glass eyes; bendable; mint; 1960s.

Marks: None

Price: $295

CHAPTER XVII

SCHUCO MONKEY

11 inches

Black, gray and white mohair; velour hands and feet; black and white googly eyes; hard and soft stuffed; all jointed; mint; circa 1960.

Marks: None

Price: $125

STEIFF *PONX* TIGER IN CAGE BOX

7 inches

Realistic striped clothing; dralon; green plastic eyes; soft and hard stuffed; mint; rare to find with original box and booklet; circa 1968.

Marks: Incised button; chest tag; presentation box and booklet

Price: $175-$185

WILD ANIMALS

STEIFF *TRAMPY* ELEPHANT
11 inches

Trevira velvet plastic eyes; felt tusks; firmly stuffed; mint; circa 1975.

Marks: Incised button; split chest tag; hang tag

Price: $145-$155

STEIFF *BAGHEERA* PANTHER
10 inches

Black acrylic plush; white inset snout; yellow plastic eyes; soft stuffed; made in 1979-1982 in the second set of the *Jungle Book Animals*; hardest to find of animals in either series; ©Disney Enterprises; tissue mint.

Marks: Brass button; split chest tag; booklet

Price: $325-$335

STEIFF *SHERE KHAN*
14 inches

One of the animals from the Jungle Book, ©Disney Enterprises; dralon; cotton and excelsior stuffed; plastic eyes; swivel head; near mint; ©Disney Enterprises; circa 1986.

Marks: None

Price: $350-$375

LEOPARD CUB

16 inches

Plush; plastic eyes; Tony Toys, England; 1980s-1990s.

Marks: Seam tag

Price: $90

CAMEL

40+ inches

Plush animal for children to lounge on; cord and tassel neck ornament; made by Dakin; 1990s.

Marks: Seam tag; leather hang tag.

Price: $350

WILD ANIMALS

REINDEER
12 inches

Plush; velour antlers and pads; sweater; Boyds Bears; 1990s.

Marks: Seam tag; hang tag

Price: $35

TWIGS GIRAFFE

Mottled gold and brown plus; birthday May 19, 1995

Marks: Ty hang tag; label

BONGO MONKEY

Brown and tan plush; birthday August 17, 1995

Marks: Ty hang tag; label

PECAN

Brown plush; birthday April 15, 1999

Marks: Ty hang tag; label

ACCESSORIES AND DISPLAY • CHAPTER XVIII

Studio animals were originally used by toy departments to attract store customers. They still are, of course, but if room is no problem they surely make a statement amongst a personal collection.

CHAD VALLEY DISPLAY TEDDY BEAR
46 inches

Brown mohair; clipped snout area; glass eyes; felt pads; excelsior stuffed; all jointed; 1920s.

Marks: Label on foot

Price: $1,900 up

STEIFF STUDIO *DALLY* DALMATION

25 inches

Mohair; glass eyes; excelsior stuffed; collar; 1950s

Marks: Raised script button; chest tag

Price: $800 and up

STEIFF NOAH'S ARK

Canvas, wood and plaster; two palm trees and ramp; small animals not included; 1950s.

Marks: None

Price: $1,000 up

BOOK: DOLLS HOUSE

Bancroft and Company, London; Spiral bound; pages open to reveal a four room dimensional doll house; told in verse form; features dolls, teddies and gollies; circa 1950.

Price: $150

STEIFF WOODEN TOY BOX

18 inches

Features Bear, Cocker and logo on lid; excellent condition; 1950s.

Marks: Logo as stated

Price: $325

STEIFF STUDIO WILD BOAR

24 inches

Tipped plush; mohair snout; glass eyes; plastic tusks; excelsior stuffed; circa 1965.

Marks: Raised script button

Price: $495-$500

ACCESSORIES AND DISPLAY

MERRYTHOUGHT *HIGHLANDER* TEDDY BEAR

36 inches

Gold mohair head and paws; plastic eyes; swivel head; made-on Scottish kilt ensemble of velvet and cotton; finely detailed; short production; few made in this size; 1980s.

Marks: Label on foot

Price: $1,400 up

STEIFF STUDIO SCREECH OWL

12 inches

Acrylic and cotton blend; beautifully airbrushed large yellow plastic eyes; soft plastic beak; double weight felt feet; soft stuffed; tissue mint; 1982.

Marks: Brass button; red studio chest tag

Price: $265

INDEX • TEDDY BEAR COMPANION—VOLUME III

A
Adebar 164
Aetna 6
Alice 219
Alresford Bears 102, 204, 205, 237
American Bears 14-19, 22-24, 27-32, 36, 37, 40-42, 51, 63, 84
Anxiety Bear 149
Applause 105
Apple Bear 200
Arco 189, 190
Atomizer Bear 137
Atomizer Cat 136
Aunt Lucy 119

B
Badgers 225
Bagheera 264
Baker and Bigler 131
Bandsmen Bears 196, 197
Bat 223
Bazi 189
Beanie Babies 107-109, 150, 179, 193, 246, 266
Bear Brand 135
Beavers 244
Berlex Bear 76
Bialosky Bear 201
Biggie 193
Bigo Belo 94
Bing Bears and Animals 21, 22, 27, 29, 35, 41, 46-48, 151, 153, 184, 250
Bingie Bears 67, 198
Birds 164-169
Bongo 266

Bonzo 185
Brent, Wendy 123
Boston, Wendy 235, 236
Bruin Bears 17, 23
Bruno 193
Bull 162
Bully Bears 98
Bully 184

C
Camel 248, 259-261, 265
Cappy 216
Cats 170-179, 214
Chad Valley Bears and Animals 55, 61, 63, 71, 72, 76, 85, 86, 88, 171, 182, 254, 267
Chameleon 232
Cheeky 90-92, 94, 96, 199
Chiltern Bears 65, 71, 72, 87
Chicken 166
Chinese Bears 98
Clancy Collectibles 98
Clark, Kathi 116
Clemens Bears 89, 94
Clown Bears 104
Clown, Schuco 155
Cocker Spaniel 185
Coco 257
Collies 191
Compact Bear 140
Compact Dog 141, 142
Convention Bear 110
Cosy Koala 236
Cow 249
Cramer Bears 49, 138
Crow 165, 166
Crowe, Nancy 124

Cubby Bear 55
Curley Bear 109
Cyrano de Bearjerac 207

D
Dachshounds 189, 214, 268
Dakin 101, 148, 265
Dally 268
Dalmatian 183, 268
Dean's Bears and Animals 64, 84, 96, 103, 183, 233, 243
Determined Production Bear 104
Diem Bears 80, 81
Diggy 225
Dismal Desmond 183
Dog Purse 146
Dogs 180-193
Doll House Book 269
Donkey 158
Ducks 162-164, 247
Dutch Bear 61
Dwarves 212, 213, 215, 217

E
Ears Rabbit 232
Eeyore 160, 161
Eden 200
Electric Eye Bears 132
Elephants 239-241, 253, 254, 256, 260, 264
Elfi 231
Embroidered Bear 142
Eric 223

F
Farnell Bears and

INDEX

Animals 38, 39, 52, 53, 57, 65, 66, 73, 87, 173, 239
Fawn 231
Fechter Bears 95
Felix 238
Ferdy 161
Festival Bears 110
Finch 167
Flamingo 169
Flask 136
Fleece 162
Floppity 232
Fox 220, 221, 226, 232
Fox Terrier 187
Frank 111, 120
Franks, Gloria 128
Franzi 168
Frogs 153, 245, 246

G

Gebhardt, Mary Ann 129
Geese 165
Giraffes 266
Goat 160, 161
Goofy 217
Graham, Ronwyn 126, 129, 130
Gran'Pop 254
Grisly Bears 97, 146, 228
Guardsmen Bears 198, 200, 202, 204
Gucki 215
Gund Bears 105, 106, 201

H

Hansi 252
Hansili 211
Harley Davidson

Bear 149
Harrison, Dickie 126
Harrod's Bear 98, 105
Hecla Bears 18
Helvetic Bears and Animals 49, 59, 61, 172
Hen 165
Hermann, Gebr. Bears and Animals 81, 90, 99, 100, 115, 118, 201, 214, 225
Hermann Spielwaren Bears 112, 120, 209
Hexie 189
Hide-A-Gift 148, 240
Highlander 207, 270
Hissy 232
Hˆrni 229
Horse 161, 251
Hucky 165, 166

I

Ideal Bears 15, 19, 22, 23, 30, 36, 120, 145
Iggy Iguana 232
Inchworm 162

J

Jabberwocky 219
Janus 144
Japanese Bears 77, 93
Jolly Skunk 242
Jopi Bears 49, 70, 134
Jubilee Bears 110, 114

K

Kamar Toy Company Bear 77
Kangaroo 262
Kersa 173, 174, 223, 224

Kesling, Debbie 129
Kilby, Kelli 126
Knickerbocker 62, 95, 146
Koala Bears 226, 227

L

Lady 192
Lady Bug 225
Lambs 159, 162, 252
Lasting Endearments 125
Lea 260
Leopard 265
Lion 260
Little Folk Bears 206
Llama 257
Loch Ness Monster 243
Lucie 212
Lucki 215

M

Macki 215
Maple 109
Marvelous Cat 173
McPherson, Donna 67, 127, 128
Mecki 215
Mediate, Flora 123
Merrythought 66-69, 90-92, 94, 96, 103, 114, 117, 119, 146, 148, 160, 173, 178, 191, 198-200, 202, 203, 206, 207, 254, 255, 261
Mickey Mouse 211, 213, 219
Micki 215
Millennium 111
Misha 148
Mobiles 168

272

Molly 184
Monkey 153, 254, 255-257, 262, 263, 266
Moose 227
Moritz Pappe 60, 61
Mouse 216
Mucki 215
Muff 134, 146
Muffy 208
Musical 49, 59, 61, 70, 83, 86, 100, 117, 134, 138, 157, 172
Muzzle Bear 26
Myers, Nancy 126
Mystic Unicorn 150

N
Nagy 244
Navy Goat 160
Nett, Gary 122
Nightdress Case 148
Nikili 214
Nikolas 210, 218
Nisbet 98, 206
Noah's Ark 268

O
Orsi 79
Oskar 214
Ostrich 169
Ooloo 171
Otter 246
Ott, Heidi 208
Owl 270

P
Paddington 118, 203
Pajama Bag 148, 191
Panda Bears 223-237
Pandy 234
Panther 264

Parakeet 168
Parrot 168
Patric 4
Patriot Bear 202
Patti 150
Peace 108
Peacock 69
Pecan 266
Peck Peck 166
Pelican 167
Pedigree 234, 242
Penguin 244
Perfume Bear 136, 144
Perfume Dwarf 137
Perfume Monkey 139
Perfume Rabbit 139
Perri 230
Peter 140
Petsy 59, 60
Petz 143
Piccy 167
Piglet 218
Pigs 159
Pinky 169
Platypus 150
Polar Bears 236, 237
Ponx 263
Poodles 187, 188, 191
Port, Beverly 121, 122
Pounce 179
Prance 179
Princess 109
Pucki 215
Puffer 169
Puffin 169
Pugsly 193
Punkinhead 88
Purse 133, 146
Puss In Boots 135, 174

Q
Quackers 162

R
Rabbits 152, 155, 221, 223, 224, 226, 227, 228, 229, 231, 232
Raccoons 232
Rag Sheet 133
Raikes, Robert 105
Rainbow 232
Record Peter 251
Reindeer 258, 261, 266
Renny 258, 261
Richard Steiff 4, 9
Ringo 232
Robby 245
Rocky 161
Rod Bear 13
Roly Poly 24
Roosevelt Bears 14, 17, 18
Rooster 167
Rough Rider 17, 195
Rupert 196, 199, 242
Russ Berrie 203

S
Sandy 216
Santa 200
Schoonmaker, Pat 103
Schuco 50, 56-58, 83, 89, 94, 136, 137, 140, 141, 143, 144, 153-157, 166, 174, 186, 192, 198, 212, 213, 216, 217, 225-229, 244, 245, 252, 255, 256, 260, 262, 263
Scotty 186, 190
Seal 245
Seaweed 246
Shakesbear 207

INDEX

Shere Kahn 264
Siamese 172, 177
Sieverling, Helen 100
Sly 232
Smardy 240
Smokey Bear 145
Smoochy 246
Snake 232
Snip 179
Snort 162
Snow Crop 145
Sooty 85
Spidy 223
Spiegel, Linda 116
Spitz 186
Squirrels 222, 225, 229, 230
St. Bernard 248
St. Nicholas 210
Steiff Bears and Animals 5-7, 20, 21, 24, 25, 33, 43, 59, 60, 78, 79, 93, 101, 106, 108, 110-115, 117, 150, 154, 159, 161, 163-169, 170, 172, 175-177, 180, 181, 184-193, 210-216, 219, 221-223, 225-227, 229-231, 234-236, 239-242, 244-246, 247-252, 253-255, 257-261, 263-265, 268-270

Stork 164
Stretch 169
Strunz 43, 194
Striuwwelpeter 218
Swapl 159
Swan 169

T

Tara 89
Teddy Baby 106, 115
Teddy Dolls 131, 132
Teddy Edward 147
Teddy Toy Co. 53
Terry, Wm. J. 35, 54, 57, 58
Tessie 188
Thumper 227
Tige 181
Tiger 255, 258, 259, 261, 262-264
Tigger 258, 261
Tom Cat 178
Toyland Bears 97
Tramp 192
Trampy 264
Treff 185
Tulla 165
Turtle 245, 246
Twigs 266
Twisty Bears 199

U

Unicorn 150

V

Valentino 107
Vera 212
Vermont Teddy Bear Co. 107

W

Waldili 214
Walther 191
Wittie 168
Wooley, Pamela 127
Wright, R. John 119, 218

Y

Yo Yo 143

Z

Zip 149
Zotty Bears 79, 100